# HARPER'S

## NEW YORK AND ERIE RAIL-ROAD

# GUIDE BOOK:

CONTAINING

A DESCRIPTION OF THE SCENERY, RIVERS TOWNS, VILLAGES, AND MOST IMPORTANT WORKS ON THE ROAD.

WITH ONE HUNDRED AND THIRTY-SIX ENGRAVINGS

BY LOSSING AND BARRITT,

FROM ORIGINAL SKETCHES MADE EXPRESSLY FOR THIS WORK

BY WILLIAM MACLEOD.

**Reprinted by New York History Review
Elmira, New York**

NEW YORK:

HARPER & BROTHERS, PUBLISHERS,
82 CLIFF STREET.

*Harper's New York and Erie Railroad Guide Book of 1851*
by William MacLeod
Reprinted by New York History Review


Copyright ©2014 New York History Review. Some rights reserved.
For more information, visit our website NewYorkHistoryReview.com


ISBN-10:0983848750
ISBN-13:978-0-9838487-5-2


Entered, according to Act of Congress, in the year one thousand
eight hundred and fifty-one, by
HARPER & BROTHERS,
in the Clerk's Office of the District Court of the Southern District
of New York.

# LIST OF ILLUSTRATIONS.

| No | | Page |
|---|---|---|
| 1. | Piermont, from the Hudson | 15 |
| 2. | Works at Piermont | 16 |
| 3. | View at Piermont, looking east | 19 |
| 4. | View at Piermont, looking north | 20 |
| 5. | Station at Blauveltville, looking east | 21 |
| 6. | View looking toward Thom's Cottage | 22 |
| 7. | Thom's Cottage, near Clarkstown, looking north | 23 |
| 8. | Suffern's Station | 24 |
| 9. | Intrenchments near Suffern's | 26 |
| 10. | Washington's Head-quarters, Suffern's, looking west | 27 |
| 11. | The Torn Mountain, from the road, looking northeast | 28 |
| 12. | Ramapo Works, Station on the left | 29 |
| 13. | Ramapo, from the Bridge, looking west | 31 |
| 14. | Station at Sloatsburg | 32 |
| 15. | Mountain Stream and Ruin with an Arch | 34 |
| 16. | Monroe Works, looking west | 36 |
| 17. | Turner's, looking west | 38 |
| 18. | Monroe, looking east | 39 |
| 19. | Station at Oxford, Sugar Loaf in the distance | 41 |
| 20. | Chester, looking west | 44 |
| 21. | Gray Court Meadows, from Chester | 44 |
| 22. | Sugar Loaf, from the Chester Station | 45 |
| 23. | Goshen | 46 |
| 24. | Station on the Walkill at New Hampton | 48 |
| 25. | Middletown Station | 49 |
| 26. | Middletown, from the north | 50 |
| 27. | View from Howell's | 51 |
| 28. | Eastern face of the Shawangunk, from near Otisville | 51 |
| 29. | Otisville, from the west | 52 |
| 30. | West side of Shawangunk | 53 |
| 31. | Wall Embankment near Otisville | 54 |
| 32. | Looking toward the Neversink Valley and Port Jervis | 54 |
| 33. | Cuddebackville, on the Delaware and Hudson Canal, looking north | 55 |
| 34. | Thorough Cut near Port Jervis | 55 |
| 35. | View near the Slate Rock Cutting, looking north | 56 |
| 36. | The Neversink, Port Jervis in the distance | 57 |
| 37. | Bridge at Port Jervis | 59 |
| 38. | Port Jervis | 59 |

vi                     LIST OF ILLUSTRATIONS.

| No. | | Page |
|---|---|---|
| 39. | Approach to the Station at Delaware, looking west | 60 |
| 40. | Station at Delaware, looking northwest | 60 |
| 41. | Canal Bridge near Port Jervis | 63 |
| 42. | Approach to the Bridge over the Canal | 63 |
| 43. | From the Bridge over the Canal, near the Glass-house Rocks | 63 |
| 44. | Saw-mill Rift Bridge, with Canal, looking north | 64 |
| 45. | From Saw-mill Rift Bridge, looking west | 64 |
| 46. | Saw-mill Rift Rocks, near the Bridge, looking east | 65 |
| 47. | Near the Great Bridge on the Delaware | 65 |
| 48. | View from Stairway Brook Station, Delaware and Hudson Canal | 67 |
| 49. | Approach to Pond Eddy, with Canal | 69 |
| 50. | Rock Cutting on the Delaware | 70 |
| 51. | The great Rock Cutting near Shohola | 71 |
| 52. | Piece of great Rock Cutting near Shohola, looking south | 72 |
| 53. | Rock Cutting near Shohola | 73 |
| 54. | Rock Cutting near Shohola, looking west | 73 |
| 55. | Bridge over the Shohola | 73 |
| 56. | From Shohola Bridge toward Barryville | 74 |
| 57. | Barryville, from Shohola Station | 75 |
| 58. | Delaware Bridge | 76 |
| 59. | Delaware Bridge Station | 77 |
| 60. | Narrowsburgh, looking west | 77 |
| 61. | Narrowsburgh, from the opposite side of the Delaware, looking north | 78 |
| 62. | Bridge on the Delaware at Narrowsburgh | 79 |
| 63. | Cochecton, from the Station, looking east | 82 |
| 64. | Cochecton, looking west | 82 |
| 65. | Station at Calicoon, looking west | 84 |
| 66. | On the Calicoon, Delaware in the distance, looking south | 85 |
| 67. | Hankin's Station | 88 |
| 68. | A rafting Station near Hankin's | 89 |
| 69. | From Equinunk Station | 90 |
| 70. | Equinunk, from the road | 91 |
| 71. | Stockport | 92 |
| 72. | On the Delaware, near the junction of its branches, below Chehocton | 93 |
| 73. | East Branch of the Delaware, near Chehocton, looking east | 93 |
| 74. | Station at Chehocton | 94 |
| 75. | Chehocton, from the road above the Station | 95 |
| 76. | West Branch of the Delaware after leaving Chehocton, looking south | 97 |
| 77. | West Branch of the Delaware, looking west | 97 |
| 78. | Near Cochecton | 97 |
| 79. | The approach to Deposit, from the east | 98 |
| 80. | Deposit Station, looking west | 98 |
| 81. | Deposit, from the west | 99 |

## LIST OF ILLUSTRATIONS.

| No. | | Page |
|---|---|---|
| 82. | Beginning to ascend Summit from Deposit | 100 |
| 83. | Gravel Bank, four miles from Deposit | 101 |
| 84. | Near the Gravel Bank, four miles from Deposit, looking west | 101 |
| 85. | Curved Embankment near the Gravel Pit | 102 |
| 86. | Half way between Summit and Deposit | 102 |
| 87. | Scene near Gulf Summit, looking north | 103 |
| 88. | Great Cut at Gulf Summit, from the east | 103 |
| 89. | From the top of Summit, Snow effect | 104 |
| 90. | Cutting at Summit, from the west | 106 |
| 91. | Cascade Bridge, from the east | 107 |
| 92. | Cascade Bridge, from below | 108 |
| 93. | West Abutment of Cascade Bridge | 109 |
| 94. | Cascade Bridge, from the Quarry, looking south | 109 |
| 95. | Cascade Bridge, from the opposite side of the River | 111 |
| 96. | First View of Susquehanna, beyond Cascade Bridge | 113 |
| 97. | First View of the Starrucca Viaduct, from the east | 115 |
| 98. | The Starrucca Viaduct, looking west | 116 |
| 99. | The Starrucca Viaduct, from the opposite side of the Susquehanna | 117 |
| 100. | Lanesborough, and Trestle Bridge | 118 |
| 101. | Starrucca, from the west | 119 |
| 102. | View of the Starrucca, Lanesborough, Trestle Bridge, &c., from above the Rail-road | 121 |
| 103. | The Works at Susquehanna, from the Station | 123 |
| 104. | Double Bridge over the Susquehanna at Lanesborough | 124 |
| 105. | Looking west to the first Rock Cutting near Great Bend | 125 |
| 106. | Distant View of the Rock Cutting near Great Bend | 125 |
| 107. | Great Rock Cutting near Great Bend | 125 |
| 108. | On the Susquehanna, looking toward Great Bend | 126 |
| 109. | Station at Great Bend, looking west | 126 |
| 110. | Village of Great Bend, from the Station, looking south | 127 |
| 111. | Station at Binghamton, from the east | 129 |
| 112. | Binghamton, from the Bridge | 130 |
| 113. | Bridges on the Chenango and Susquehanna, looking north | 131 |
| 114. | From the Bridge over the Chenango, looking north | 133 |
| 115. | Union, from the Station | 136 |
| 116. | View looking toward Union, from the west | 137 |
| 117. | Bridge over the Susquehanna near Campville, looking north | 138 |
| 118. | Station at Campville | 139 |
| 119. | Owego, from the Road | 139 |
| 120. | Station at Owego, looking west | 140 |
| 121. | Owego, from the Station, looking south | 140 |
| 122. | Smithborough, looking west | 142 |
| 123. | Cut near Barton | 143 |
| 124. | Barton, from the old road | 143 |
| 125. | Straight Section between Barton and Waverley, looking northwest | 143 |
| 126. | Waverley | 144 |

viii  LIST OF ILLUSTRATIONS.

| No. | | Page |
|---|---|---|
| 127. | Station at Waverley, looking west | 144 |
| 128. | Station at Waverley, Spanish Hill | 145 |
| 129. | On the Chemung | 147 |
| 130. | On the Chemung | 147 |
| 131. | Gravel Cut near Wellsburg, looking east | 148 |
| 132. | Rocky Cut near Wellsburg | 148 |
| 133. | Station at Elmira | 149 |
| 134. | Elmira, from the west | 151 |
| 135. | Corning, from the opposite side of the Chemung | 157 |
| 136. | Painted Post, from the east | 158 |
| | NY & E Railroad Map | 174 |
| | Table of Distances | 177 |

# PREFACE.

The object of this work is to furnish the traveler on the New York and Erie Rail-road with that kind of information which every one passing over a new route desires to have in his possession. In securing this, we not only add to the pleasures of rail-road traveling, but relieve it of much of the tediousness which is so often the companion of a long ride.

The work, it is hoped, will find favor not only with travelers, but with those who take an interest in the progress of internal improvements, of which our road is one of the most important, being the longest rail-road owned by one company and under one management in the world.

The engravings form a prominent feature of the book. The sketches for them, as well as the accompanying descriptions, were all furnished expressly for this work by Mr. William MacLeod, and, with the exception of two or three, have never before been published. They are intended to be *portraits* of the scenery and objects represented.

New York, April, 1851.

# ILLUSTRATED GUIDE-BOOK

OF THE

# NEW YORK AND ERIE RAIL-ROAD.

---

BEFORE introducing a friend to a distinguished stranger, it is advisable to give him some account of the person whose acquaintance he is about to make; and so, fellow-traveler, whom I introduce to the NEW YORK AND ERIE RAIL-ROAD, it may be well to prefix here a brief sketch of the history and present condition of this, the *Lion of Railways*. True, he is yet in an unfinished state, but you will find that what there is of him is complete, and of wondrous organization and activity. His magnificent head and front repose in grandeur on the shores of the Hudson; his iron lungs puff vigorously among the Highland fastnesses of Rockland; his capacious maw "fares sumptuously" on the dairies of Orange, and the game and cattle of Broome; his *lumbar region* is built upon the timber of Chemung, and the tuft of his royal extremity floats triumphantly on the waters of Lake Erie. In plain words, we will record briefly the origin, progress, and history of the road.

In connection with the internal improvement system of New York, many curious facts may be found by looking into the Statute-book of the Colony of New York—instructive as to the beginning of the great rail-road and canal system which is now nearly completed, and, from the various connections between the port of New York and the Lakes, ultimately to be extended to the Pacific Ocean. In the *time of Queen Anne*, the Assembly of the

Colony of New York appropriated the sum of £500 to John Smith and some other persons for the purpose of constructing a public road leading from New York to the West, and the appropriation was coupled with the conditions that within two years from the time of the passage of the act the beneficiaries should have constructed the road, wide enough for two carriages to pass, from "Nyack on the Hudson River to Sterling Iron-works," a distance of twenty or thirty miles; and that they should cut away the limbs of trees over the track, so as to allow the carriages to pass. That was the beginning of the internal improvement system of the State of New York, which, after the lapse of more than one hundred and twenty years, has proceeded no further than to open a canal and two rail-roads, one of which is completed, and the other nearly so, from the city of New York to Lake Erie.

The Legislature of New York, at their session of 1825 (the Erie Canal having been opened in 1824), directed a survey of a "State Road," to be constructed at the public expense, through the southern tier of counties, from the Hudson River to Lake Erie. The unfavorable profile exhibited in the survey, the discordant views and interests, resulted in the abandonment of the project. The subject did not, however, cease to occupy the attention of many, and the manifest and growing benefits of the canal did but increase the conviction in the southern tier of counties of the importance and necessity to them of an equivalent thoroughfare.

At length "THE NEW YORK AND ERIE RAIL-ROAD COMPANY" was incorporated by the Legislature, on the 24th of April, 1832, with power to construct a rail-road from the city of New York, or some point near, to Lake Erie, to transport persons and property thereon, and to regulate their own charges for transportation. Since that period, every succeeding year has added to the force of all the considerations in favor of such a thoroughfare; the population, trade, and wealth of this city, and of this and the Western States, and the intercourse between New York and the region of the Lakes, have been vastly augmented; and the necessity of greater facilities for constant and rapid communication throughout the whole year have become more and more evident, especially since the means of such communication have been in progress on several more southerly routes, between the waters of the Atlantic and the Ohio River.

No survey of the route had been made prior to the act of incorporation; but in the summer of 1832, a *reconnoissance* was conducted, under the authority of the government of the United States, by Col. De Witt Clinton, Jr., which resulted in presenting strong inducements for obtaining a more complete and accurate instrumental survey of the whole line.

In 1833, $1,000,000 was subscribed to the capital stock, and the company organized in August for active operations, by the election of directors and officers. In 1834, an appropriation for the survey of the route was made by the Legislature, to be conducted under the authority of the state government, and Governor Marcy appointed Benjamin Wright, Esq., to conduct the survey. During the year, a survey was made of the whole line, 483 miles in length, and complete maps and profiles, with the report and estimates of Judge Wright, were deposited in the office of the Secretary of State.

At the time this report was made, much was said in the Legislature and in the public prints to discourage the undertaking "as chimerical, impracticable, and useless." The road, it was declared, could never be made, and, if made, would never be used. The southern counties were asserted to be mountainous, sterile, and worthless, affording no products requiring a road to market, or if they did, that they ought to resort to the Valley of the Mohawk as their natural outlet!

The favorable results of the state survey dispelled all reasonable doubts of the feasibility of the improvement, and measures were taken preparatory to further and more active operations. An additional amount was subscribed to the capital stock, amounting, with the previous subscription, to $2,362,100. The entire route was resurveyed in 1836, and a part of the road located and commenced.

But the commercial revulsion and universal derangement of the currency of the country about the close of 1836 occasioned a suspension of the work until 1838, when the Legislature modified the law of 1836, granting to the company, in aid of its construction, a loan of the credit of the state for $3,000,000. At the session of the Legislature in 1840, the Loan Bill was further amended, and this, together with the collections on the stock subscriptions, enabled the company to locate and vigorously prosecute the work on a distance of 300 miles of the road.

The first portion, a section of 46 miles, from Piermont to Goshen, was put in operation on the 23d of September, 1841. In 1842, under its complicated embarrassments, arising from the nature and amount of its indebtedness, the affairs of the company were placed in the hands of assignees. After encountering many obstacles and embarrassments attending and following the suspension of the work, and after various efforts to obtain the means necessary to extricate the company from its difficulties, and to a resumption of the work, the law was passed by the Legislature, 14th of May, 1845, relating to the construction of the road, the release of the state claim, subscriptions to the stock, &c. The Board of Directors (at present mostly in control of the road) entered upon the discharge of their responsible duties of resuscitating a work which is destined to add permanent wealth and prosperity to the city and state, and presented a plan to the public which placed the work in a position to be successfully prosecuted to completion. The appeal was responded to by the merchants and business men of New York, and the subscription of $3,000,000 to the capital stock was speedily filled up. Successive portions of the road were put in operation from time to time, until it now stretches across the whole state, from the Hudson to Lake Erie, three hundred miles into the interior, producing results beyond the most sanguine expectation of its early friends. A considerable portion of the country traversed by the route, without being mountainous, has an undulating surface, intersected throughout nearly its whole extent by a chain or series of rivers, pursuing, with little deviation, the general line of direction of the route of the road. Those streams are free from sudden falls, flowing at a gentle rate of descent, seldom exceeding fifteen, and frequently less than two feet to the mile, and presenting on their margins alluvial flats, interrupted in a few cases (principally on the Delaware) by projecting bluffs.

With these preliminary hints of the road we are to travel, let us now step aboard of the "Thomas Powell," lying at the company's pier at the foot of Duane Street. This wharf is covered with a substantial wooden tenement, 300 feet in length, for the protection of the freight intrusted to the company; and, owing to the constant increase of business, growing with the extension of the road, this vast shed always contains piles of the productions brought down from its various sections. Milk-cans, strawberry-baskets, butter-tubs, and immense deer lie in heaps, the representatives of their different regions; and, in exchange for these, there are the *luxuries* destined for the inland towns and sequestered hamlets, which the railroad now dispenses so rapidly. Three fine steamers for the transmission of passengers to the eastern terminus of the road at Piermont are provided, one of which is designed for winter use, when the river is frozen. Besides these, the company runs a *milk-boat*, employed in bringing down to New York the lacteal supplies from the region to which the Erie Rail-way is now the only outlet. This staple is brought to New York at midnight, and at day-break those myriad cans "pair off," and are seen flanking the young Jehus that fly through the streets of Gotham in light wagons, calling out, with their unearthly shrieks, red-elbowed house-maids to receive their daily allowance from those huge urns. Our own boat, you perceive, has her forecastle piled up with the discharged cans, that now are tossed about and battered, though this very night, as they descend *full* again, each will enjoy the reserved right of every tub or other vessel "to stand on its own bottom." At present they look as useless and degraded as empty champaign-bottles. But we are off from the pier, on our way up stream.

We have heard much of the absurdity of the Erie Railroad terminating so far up the Hudson, and not at Jersey City or Hoboken; but, whatever be the inconvenience, delay, or unpleasantness of the sail to Piermont during winter, commend us to this same voyage on a bright summer morning, when we are refreshed by the cool puffs of the river air, amused with the ever-animated scenes on its surface, and then descend with a will and an appetite to a comfortable breakfast. A cigar and the morning papers having succeeded that hearty meal, we promenade the deck, and stare for the thousandth time at the basaltic wonder of the Palisades, then at the opposite wonder of Mr. Forest's castle, with its heavy "box entrance," and, just as we begin to weary with the sail, lo! before us the broad basin of the Tappan Zee, on the west side of which runs, far out into the blue tide, the bright yellow line of the *Pier* that gives the name to the point where we take the rail for the West. The distance of this point from New York is 24 miles. The view of Piermont and its pier from the river is very beautiful. Over the long, flat extent of the latter, with its freight-houses, trains, and

crowds of passengers and workmen, the village makes a pretty show, while the steep heights above are dotted with pretty cottages, amid gardens and cedar-groves. To the left the hill-sides slope suddenly into a glen, up which lies the course of the New York and Erie Rail-road. The left side of this valley presents a beautiful wooded hill, descending to the wide, yellow, marshy flats extending far out into the river south of the pier. Nature seems to have selected this point for an ingress through the steep sides of the Hudson to the country beyond, for the long, pillared wall of the Palisades here suddenly sinks into a ravine of gentle slope, to swell again abruptly into a mountainous range, that assumes a grander form in the bold Nyack hills to the north of Piermont.

The pier we have now gained affords a sample of the vast extent and costliness of the New York and Erie Railroad. Extending one mile in length, it presents a general width of 50 feet, expanding, at its river extremity, into a fine front 300 feet wide, within which there is a spacious basin or dock, affording safe accommodation for the company's boats. A large wooden depôt for cars, stores, and freight stands at their extremity, and under its projecting eaves the trains receive their passengers and goods. The surface of this vast pier is cut up with tracks and "switches" without number, along whose iron veins circulates unceasingly the noisy life-blood of a great rail-way depôt. The cost of the pier has been large, for not only is its causeway *made* ground, but also the wide area at its base, which has been *filled in* for the erection of the offices, work-shops, and stations where we now stop. Arrangements having been made by the company by which passengers to and from the West take the shorter route through New Jersey, this vast depôt ground, with its buildings, will be devoted almost exclusively to the accommodation of the immense freighting business of the road.

Here we can form some idea of the energy and enterprise of the company in establishing a spacious depôt at Piermont, where otherwise was not room for a single track to run along the steep river-shore. On the north side of the area are workshops. These may be consid-

ered the *stables* and *stud* that supplies the high-way before us with its iron steeds; and a few items about their extent may not be tiresome to those curious in the statistics of such a road. Persons are constantly exclaiming about the wonders of a rail-*road*. Let them enter its work-shops, and see the "mighty heart" whose pulsations cause the long track to beat in healthy order through a distance of 450 miles! For this reason, fellow-traveler, hear some items of the economy of Vulcan's head-quarters at Piermont.

For the whole extent of the Erie road, including its branches, there are used at present over 100 engines, keeping in employ more than 350 men and 40 furnaces. There are about seventy employed in the machine department, in which every thing pertaining to the steam-engine can be made and repaired. In the car-shop there is a force of about eighty men, that last year, in addition to all the repairs, turned out 200 freight, baggage, and passenger cars, the upholstery and painting of which were also done by hands employed here. In addition to these, there are the engine-houses, with room for 28 engines. Ritchie has well said that "the movements of a great rail-way require to be governed with as much precision as those of a great army;" and, truly, an examination of the head-quarters at Piermont, inside and out, will show the grand scale of the operations that regulate the marching and counter-marching on the Erie road. With these matter-of-fact details we will "lump" a few others about the track itself that may be interesting. The New York and Erie Rail-road has a track of fine width of what is called the *six feet gauge*, considered the best and safest of all others. The T rail is used through its entire length, and weighs about 55 to 60 pounds to the yard. These together give a remarkably easy and steady motion to the cars, while the wide gauge affords ample room for luxurious accommodations for passengers.

We will now quit the dingy precincts of Vulcan, and take a look at

PIERMONT (from the pier one mile).—The embankment on which the station stands divides the prettily-situated village into two parts. That to the north of us is the main business street, facing the work-shops, and showing along its entire length neat stores, dwellings, a church, and a large hotel, that gives it an air of dignity and importance. Above rise the steep mountains, up which, as we have said, are scattered beautiful cottages, with now and then an elegant mansion among trees. Many of these *up-town* dwellings are occupied during summer by city folks, that find Piermont a pleasant and convenient resort. South of the station, the village is built along the Sparkill, a small creek issuing from the valley we are soon to enter. The dwellings further up the stream are very neat and tasty, having small gardens around them. Beyond these, scattered over the yellow, marshy " flats," are numerous Irish shanties, the fast-disappearing types of what Piermont altogether was a few years ago, when it figured in the Gazetteer as a " fishing village, with considerable trade, supporting *three sloops!*" Tappan Slote was then its title—slote being, we believe, the Dutch for *ditch*, and applied to the pretty stream now called the *Sparkill*. Indeed, such squalid hovels, only two years since, offended the eye in the midst of the new and *fashionable* part of the village. Now look at the wonderful change wrought in this "fishing village" by the beneficent power of steam! The "nets" of its former "traders" are now represented by the mazy *net-work* of iron tracks upon that pier, and for the "three sloops" are substituted as many steam-boats, to say nothing of the *land*-steamers running up and down that long track, like jockies trying their steeds on a training-course. The population is estimated at over one thousand. The visitor will find it well worth his while to ascend the heights above the village, and enjoy the prospects they afford. The most striking of these is the map-like view of the station and pier, which last looks as though it ran half way across the river. Opposite is Mr. Paulding's residence at Tarrytown, and Washington Irving's country seat. The broad, placid sheet of the Hudson contrasts singularly with the noisy hive and artificial lines of the station, while on the right, just be-

neath us, winds the sinuous Sparkill among its grassy meadows. But listen how the "*Knickerbocker*" thus felicitously hits off the sights and sounds of Piermont, after describing the bright shores opposite : " Hark ! the shriek of the steam-whistle and its white breath brings us to the foreground, and we look down upon long, snaky trains of freight-cars, gliding amid a labyrinth of iron tracks, and preceded by a puffing locomotive, that often requires the application of "*a switch*" to keep it in the proper track ; upon groups and clusters of brick structures (some of them in the *pointed Ionic* style of architecture) ; upon half a mile of new cars and an acre of car-wheels ; upon the smoke of Stygian forges, whence comes up also "the clink of hammers closing rivets up," the slow, grinding noise of iron planes driven by steam-engines ; and upon ditchers "laying pipe" with as little regard for the consequences of his labor as any politician that ever performed the same labor before them !"

Northward we have a superb view of the Nyack hills, and the fine curve of the river between them and Pier-

mont, making it much resemble the Bay of Naples. The view, also, looking westward, embraces a vast landscape, through which our road passes, and on its furthermost verge we may see the *Ramapo Gap*, a very remarkable notch in the mountains of that valley, 17 miles distant.

The country around Piermont is full of historical interest associated with the Revolution. Directly opposite, and near Tarrytown, is the spot where Major Andre was arrested by the three militia-men; and at Tappan, a village three miles south of Piermont, was the scene of his execution. His grave is still pointed out, but in 1831 the body was taken to England, and deposited in Westminster Abbey. In a work descriptive of this state, published by the New York Historical Society in 1841, there is a very interesting account of the exhumation, and also of Andre's execution, as described by an *eye-witness*.

Our road leaves Piermont by a southwesterly curve round some heavy rock-cutting, and then turning westward, we ascend the valley of the Sparkill by a grade of sixty feet to the mile. This grade is necessary to attain the country beyond, and extends, with occasional levels and descents, twelve and a half miles, to Monsey. As we enter the valley near Piermont, we have a beautiful view of the Sparkill and the neat cottages lining its banks, each with its little garden, that speaks so well the happy condition of its occupant. These are the snug abodes of the artisans in the work-shops, and it is gratifying to think those sons of Vulcan have such pleasant retreats from the smoke, noise, and labor of the day. Very soon, however, this fair part of the valley, with the broad Hudson and the noisy village, are lost to sight, and we emerge upon an open country of poor soil, but abounding in orchards. A double track is laid upon this portion of the road, extending from Piermont to Clarkstown.

BLAUVELTSVILLE (from pier four and a half miles) is the first stopping-place on our way West. The track is here crossed by a substantial wooden bridge, and on the humble platform of the station you see the first pile of the "noble army" of milk-cans drawn up in imposing array on all the stations before us for sixty miles—a section of the road happily termed the "Milky Way." Though Rockland county furnishes but little of this great staple compared with that supplied by her neighbor Or-

ange, yet she almost exclusively contributes another luxury, which, when combined with the lacteal product, forms a compound of the most delicious associations. Her *strawberries* are famous for their abundance and fine flavor. According to a statement of the superintendent of the road last year, a single train took down to New York in one day 80,000 baskets of strawberries and 28,000 quarts of milk. It is estimated that the people of this county receive during the season $3000 *per diem* for that delicious fruit alone. Well does the region deserve the *strawberry-leaf* in its coronet.

At Blauveltsville the road passes through a deep cut of clay, and a mile or two further passes over a long embankment, the view from which shows the height we have attained above the river. The country here is very open, and, looking to the southeast, we can see the bold headlands of the Palisades stretching away as far as Hoboken.

CLARKSTOWN (from pier nine miles) is the second station, and is nine miles from Piermont. Here terminates the double track of the Erie road. A platform and a brick grocery, the proprietor of which is also postmaster, constitutes all to be seen at this stopping-place. This region was originally settled by Dutch Huguenots. The country in this vicinity is very uninteresting and uncultivated, and its dull aspect will make you look with the more interest upon that little brown stone Gothic cottage on the

right of the road, a mile and a half beyond Clarkstown. This architectural gem is of two stories, of elaborate design and finish, and embowered in trees of various kinds. It was built by Mr. Thom, the celebrated Scottish self-taught mason-sculptor of "Tam O'Shanter and Souter Johnnie," who resided here for some months. A life-size statue of Washington, cut by him out of a single block

of stone, stands in the garden, facing the gate. Though we think Mr. Thom's genius lay more in imbodying the humorous heroes of Burns, yet this Washington has much nobility of form and feature, is well proportioned, and, on the whole, makes a better show than most foreign attempts upon this great subject which we have seen.

Of the next two stopping-places,

SPRING VALLEY, eleven and a half miles from Piermont, and

MONSEY, thirteen miles, nothing more may be said than that they are a pair of uninteresting settlements growing up round the stations, placed in a dull-looking country. At Monsey we reach the summit of the heavy grade of sixty feet, that has lifted us from the edge of the Hudson, and enter a descending one of a like description, that extends five and a half miles beyond. Unless the traveler prefers watching the agility of the hands at the wood-pile or water-tank, studying the faces of the natives alongside of the milk-cans always drawn up on the platform, he had better take a nap while passing this region. He must be wide awake, however, after passing Monsey, for there looms directly across our path a dark curtain of mountains, rising higher and higher as we approach. The long line of its ridge is soon broken into what is called the *Ramapo Gap* (the same as seen from the heights above Piermont), and here, in its very jaws, we stop at

SUFFERN'S (from New York 32 miles, from pier 18 miles, from Dunkirk 428 miles). This station is placed at the entrance of the mountain pass, and has an imposing *setting*, of course. It is by far the most important one we have reached, and is the terminus of the Paterson and Hudson River, Paterson and Ramapo, and Union Rail-roads, that extend from Jersey City, opposite the city of New York, a distance of 31 miles.

The UNION RAIL-ROAD here connects our road with the Paterson and Ramapo and with the Paterson and Hudson River Rail-road. It extends from the station at Suffern's south to the New Jersey line, a distance of about half a mile. It is owned by an independent company, and was constructed under the provisions of the general rail-road law. The gauge is four feet ten inches, the same as the Ramapo road.

[Since the foregoing was prepared for publication, an arrangement has been entered into between the New York and Erie Rail-road Company and the Union Rail-road Company, by which the passengers coming to and from the Erie Rail-road will be carried over the Union, Ramapo, and Paterson roads to and from New York. By this arrangement, from one and a quarter to one and a half hours' time is gained. Passengers leave New York from Chambers Street pier, opposite the Erie depôt, and are taken by ferry-boat to Jersey City, where they take the cars. Along the road, for the first few miles, little of interest is to be seen. Passing through a rock-cut of considerable extent, the road runs on a straight line over the meadows, and crossing the Hackensack River by a long piled bridge, and by another bridge crosses the Passaic at the pleasant village of Acquacknonck, 12 miles from New York. Four and a half miles further on the road passes through the easterly portion of the town of Paterson. The Paterson and the Ramapo roads unite about half a mile south of the depôt in the town, to which the Paterson road runs.

Paterson is a manufacturing town of considerable importance, and has a population of 11,500. There are two extensive locomotive manufactories here, where have been built many of the engines running upon the Erie road, as well as those upon this road. From Paterson, on the Ramapo road, the traveler is whirled over a smooth track, through a country possessing no particular interest, with no villages, but well populated and tolerably cultivated, 15 miles to Suffern's station, when he exchanges the cars he came from Jersey City in for the wide and luxurious cars of the Erie Rail-road. It is probable that before long the track of the roads from Suffern's to Jersey City will be widened to correspond with the Erie, and that the same cars will run through from the Hudson River to Lake Erie.]

At Suffern's we find ourselves entering a region interesting from its romantic scenery, its abundant iron ore, its factories and mills, and its Revolutionary history. The Ramapo Valley was the only route between New York and the western counties during the Revolution. Many of Washington's letters were dated here while encamped in 1780; and this "*pass*" came near being the scene of a great struggle during that eventful period. Washington, expecting the advance of the British troops from New York and New Jersey against the American forces in the Highlands, took up a position with his army a mile and a half beyond Suffern's, and where the "pass" was not more than a quarter of a mile wide. A more formidable position could not have been selected; but the enemy did not test its impregnability. To the right of

the rail-road, and very near it, the marks of the old intrenchments are still visible in the fosse and ridge extending to the mountain to the north, and the traces of the camp-fires of our French allies are perceptible in the woods of the opposite flank. Half a mile eastward of

Suffern's, and to the north of the road, from which it is concealed, stands an old farm-house—the head-quarters

of Washington when here with his army. Though these "*head-quarters*" are indeed *legion* in some portions of the country, we regard the sneer and incredulity visited upon their claims to such an honor as highly unreasonable. Considering the length of the Revolutionary struggle, and the ever-shifting position of our forces, it is not strange that many a farm-house should thus be consecrated for all time by the presence of the commander-in-chief. The "quarters" near Suffern's can not justly be deemed apocryphal, for, being so near the intrenched army, and being a house of (for that era) stately accommodations, the *circumstantial evidence* of its having been his head-quarters is irresistible. The house is in good preservation, and occupied by a Mr. Carpenter, who hospitably entertained the writer of this in an apartment where the father of his country may have planned those campaigns that subsequently achieved our independence. This interesting relic belongs to Major Suffern, one of the chief land-holders of this region, and from whom the station derives its name. From Suffern's we ascend another light grade, extending nine miles. Beyond the old intrenchments, the rail-road crosses the *Ramapo*, a small stream that, having led a wild but very useful life as a mill-brook in the mountains, flows toward us placidly through a meadowy vale on our right. From the high embankment here there is a noble view of the mountain that forms the right shoulder of the Ramapo Gap, called the *Torn*, which word is here said to be the Dutch for *steeple*. But as you, my considerate tourist, will doubtless linger in this region, you can see this noble peak to better advantage from the small bridge over the Ramapo, a few yards north of the one we have crossed, and where we took the accompanying sketch.

The scene there is just such a one as Durand would like to paint—so perfect in its composition—a happy mixture of the gentle and the wild, the sublime and the beautiful. Standing there under that vine-hung sycamore, you see the Ramapo coming toward you through a sea of level meadow. On the right a group of beeches overshades its stream, in which cattle stand knee-deep and drowsy. On the left rises a knoll, capped by a neat cottage covered with vine, while immediately opposite and in the center "swells from the vale"—and I have no doubt "midway leaving" any "storm" that ever broke on his Titan breast, rises the rocky crest of the *Torn*—chief of the Ramapo clan! His is no monotonous mound of verdure, but he bares his rocky front, and shows it seamed and riven in successive layers, that stand out boldly in the light, and throw deep, mysterious shadows over his broad bosom. From the "steepled" peak of the *Torn*, a very extensive view, embracing even the harbor of New York, may be had for the climbing, and it is said that Washington often ascended there to watch the movements of the British fleet. On one of these excursions, we are also told, he lost his watch on the summit, and the legend has it that it is still going there *on tick!*

Following up this romantic valley, we again join the Ramapo in its narrowest gorge, where its useful waters

long since established the RAMAPO IRON-WORKS (from New York 34 miles, from Dunkirk 426 miles). This station, 19 miles from Piermont, is one of the most interesting on the road, from the picturesqueness of the scenery and the extent of the once thriving works, visible from the cars. The mountains here rise precipitously, leaving but a narrow strip of soil on one side of the river, that, dammed beyond all chance of escape, spreads out into quite a lake, affording a great water-power. These works, for rolling and splitting iron, and for manufacturing *cut nails*, were established in 1824 by a company, at the head of which was the venerable Judge Pierson, the proprietor of this territory, who has resided here since early manhood. By the enterprise of this gentleman, the valuable iron ore so abundant in the neighborhood was made available on an extensive scale. With plenty of iron and water power, the works for many years were very successful, but competition of rival establishments injured those at Ramapo, and now the amount of the business done by them is comparatively small. This was the first establishment in the county where cut nails were made. Another enterprise has proved more successful here. Two years since a manufactory of *files* was established, all the workmen and boys in which were brought from Sheffield, England, and so far it has proved very successful. A new building, on a large scale, is now being erected for the same manufacture. A large cotton-mill of brick was also established here by Judge Pierson. It was unsuccessful, and is now not in operation. It is sad to see the wreck of so many of the liberal enterprises of this gentleman, who commenced life in an humble vocation, has filled several offices of public trust, and now, in his old age, unfortunately, has not reaped the substantial rewards his exertions merited. He has, however, the satisfaction of seeing the success of the Erie Rail-road, of which, from the first, he has been the warm friend and advocate. Most of the dwellings of Ramapo stand on the stream half a mile below us, and from the bridge near the iron-works there is a very beautiful view

of the valley, the village locked in by noble hills, over all of which the *Torn* shoots up his rocky head. There is an endless variety of romantic scenery around Ramapo, and the broad expanse of the river above the dam gives a peculiar charm to the landscape, with its clear surface and the frequent pleasure-boats reflected in it.

One mile beyond Ramapo the road makes a sudden bend to the northward, and emerges upon a wide, fertile tract, though still hemmed in by a picturesque range of hills, to get out of which a stranger would be at a loss to know how to run a rail-road. From the height just above this curve, looking north, there is a superb view of the valley, in the midst of which lies, two miles from Ramapo, our next station,

SLOATSBURG (from New York 35 miles, from Dunkirk 425 miles). This beautiful and thriving place presents a singular aspect to the traveler. From the station he sees two substantial cotton factories, and not a sign of a village or hamlet in sight, the damsels employed in them dwelling in the humble but neat abodes scattered along this "happy valley." Embowered in noble trees, the mills look as though placed in a gentleman's park, did not the adjacent dingy blacksmith shop show that the precincts were those of a regular factory. This establishment was

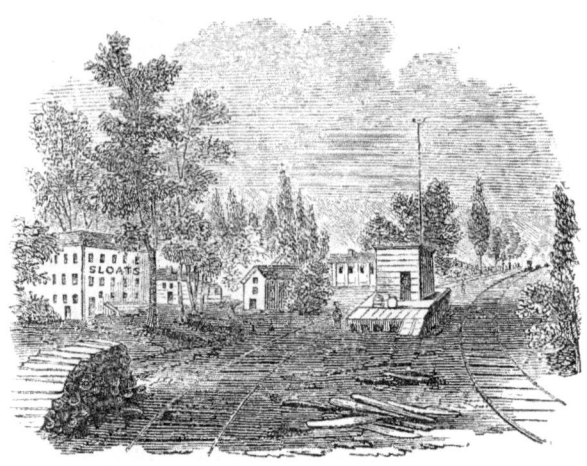

erected in 1820, the brick portion in 1846, and are used exclusively for making *cotton twine*, of which important article 5000 pounds are weekly sent "by rail" to New York. This improved twine is the invention of the principal proprietor of the mills and owner of the grounds on which they stand, Major Jacob Sloat, from whom the place gets its name. Major Sloat's enterprise and mechanical ingenuity have brought the mills to their present flourishing condition, and his good taste has made Sloatsburg the fairest portion of the valley. He derives his domain from his grandfather, to whom it was assigned by five Indian chiefs in 1738, and the original deed of conveyance is truly a literary curiosity, for, the settler being from Holland (as, indeed, were all those who originally came to this valley), the document is drawn up in a choice lingo, compounded of Dutch and Indian. If the tourist stop here, and penetrates beyond that factory and its grove, he will see evidences of the immense influence of one man's controlling taste in the well-fenced meadows, the sacred regard for trees that give the place its park-like beauty, and the general prosperous air of every dwelling around him. And what nobler certificate of character can there be than in such fair characters of neatness, order, and industry, written upon a man's estate? To accommodate his neighbors, the major has put up a "model country store," stylish enough for a country residence, from which, however, is rigidly excluded all intoxicating drinks. Judge Pierson, of Ramapo, also excludes alcohol from his estate, and thus much of the order and prosperity of the valley may be attributed to the praiseworthy prudence of these gentlemen. Strangers wishing to linger here are surprised to find there are no public houses for their accommodation, which may be owing to the indisposition of landlords to put up such without the privilege of a bar-room, so ruinous to the morals of a rural population.

At Sloatsburg the tourist can take the stage that runs thrice a week to *Greenwood Lake,* 12 miles distant—a beautiful sheet of water eight miles long, that lies on the border line between New York and Jersey. It lies romantically among steep mountains, and is the favorite resort of the "knights of the rod and line." A good hotel, also, may be found there, with plenty of boats and "tackle."

We have said the original settlers of this neighborhood were Dutch, and were generally considered opposed to all spirit of improvement. Until recently, little was known of the people beyond the limits, their anti-innovation disposition keeping them ever at home. Much of this ignorance of what is going on with their neighbors still exists. An amusing instance of it is told as occurring in an adjacent community called Johnston, where, not many years back, the panther and other wild beasts were to be found. Every one, on first hearing the present new style of steam-whistle used on the Erie Rail-road, has been startled by its unearthly hoarseness, as though it had a bad cold, a "church-yard cough," so different from its old-fashioned ear-piercing shrillness of pipe. Soon after the introduction of this asthmatic stranger in the Ramapo Valley, the village of Johnston was "frightened from its propriety" by strange, awful sounds in the forests, occurring day and night. They were at once attributed to the wild animals holding their revels in the woods. It was believed some lingering specimen of the mastodon caused the row, and therefore, one dark night, the villagers, collecting guns, axes, and pitch-forks, lay in ambuscade for the monster at the hour he selected for his vocal exercises. At the usual hour the roar was heard, and so suddenly and so near that the party were about to hurry back to their anxious wives and mothers, when, lo! through the gloom of night issued the glaring Cyclops eye of the locomotive, that treated them with another blast from his hoarse lungs as he rushed by them!

Leaving Sloatsburg, our course runs directly northward, and we are once more in the iron region, and pass several works, both in active operation and in decay. One of

these, in ruin, is the most picturesque object along the road, and merits particular notice. It is on the right side of the road (going westward), and therefore, fellow-traveler, keep a look-out, for it can be seen but for an instant. It is known as the old *Augusta Iron-works*. The road makes a sudden curve near it, and there it is right before you, the loneliest and loveliest nook imaginable. The Ramapo makes two leaps from a grove of willows, over fantastic ledges of gray rock rising perpendicularly on the right, covered with trees of every sort, and its crest bristling with hemlock. On this side of the cascade rises a knoll of darkest green verdure, and overshadowed with tall trees. A wall, mossy and crumbling, separates this knoll from a grassy slope that descends toward us and to the foot of the cascade, and on its bare greensward stands the crumbling gable of the mill, overrun and festooned with every sort of wild vine and *parasite*, in the autumn forming a matted garland of the most brilliant hues thrown over the old gray, decayed wall. The interior of the ruin is filled with a mass of broad-leaved pumpkin-vines, with their golden globes lodged among moist old mill-wheels and other *debris*, of deep rich brown earthy hues. As this ivied relic stands immediately in front of the cascade, the foam and flash of which are seen through the arched gate, while the deep, cool shadows of the ravine powerfully relieve the gay-mantled gable, the whole picture strikes the eye of the visitor as a happy one, whose interest, made up of ivied ruins and fresh, romantic brook scenery, not often seen in our country, are fully equal to one half the vaunted "ruins" we have seen in the Old World. Short as the glimpse is, we at once have visions of a picnic on that shady knoll; and while the claret cools on the edge of that mass of foam, we wander in fancy with fair damsels over that bright green turf, round the old walls of that ruin so richly draped and garlanded!

The Augusta Iron-works were very celebrated in their day, and are among the oldest in this region. The heavy chain placed across the Hudson at West Point, to check the advance of the British fleet, was forged here. Near these works the road passes through a heavy rock-cutting, and crosses the Ramapo by a substantial wooden bridge.

We now leave Rockland county and enter that of Orange, of which the former was once a part. It seems singular that the division was not made some six miles, at least, further north, where Nature herself seems to have placed a natural divorce between Vulcan and Ceres, as represented in the forges of Rockland and smiling fields of Orange. As it is, the iron god appears still to thrust his fingers through the yellow hair of the golden goddess, as you will see by the blackened chimneys that mark the road for several miles in Orange county. After crossing the Ramapo, the valley expands, though the cultivation is not such as makes Sloatsburg so beautiful. Indeed, in many places there is a primitive wildness. The eye of the observant traveler will not fail to see how gradually the mountains indicate the improvement of the soil on their side. The unbroken wall of rock and forest, that has followed us on each side from Suffern's, is becoming invaded. The plow has evidently made an assault upon those heights, and here and there, midway up, the patches of fields and an occasional hut show that permanent positions have been carried.

MONROE WORKS (from New York 42 miles, from Dunkirk 418 miles) is our next stopping-place. It takes its name from the adjacent iron-works that once flourished

here, but are now greatly reduced in point of work, exhibiting another sample of that most desolate of all objects, a ruined mill; its huge joints, sinews, and ribs, so evidently made for "hard labor," now lying ill, or in but weakly condition, like a giant in consumption! This is the last of Vulcan's work-shops we shall see, though there are many others in the neighborhood. The ore used in the Monroe Works is brought from mines six miles off, and is said to be the best in the country for *cannon*. In taking leave of these iron-works, we must say a word about the useful little stream which, for near a century, has fed them with its tide. The word *Ramapo* is Indian, and is said to mean the "*river of round ponds*," thus describing the peculiarity of its origin from the numerous ponds among the hill-tops already spoken of. Ramapo, thus made up of the surplus waters of these singular mountain basins, runs through the valley, and, after being "*broken on the wheel*" by the numerous mills along its banks, closes its well-spent life in the bosom of the Passaic, in Jersey.

A spacious hotel, kept by Mr. Coffee, near Monroe Works station, affords good accommodations to those wishing to spend the summer in that quiet region, and to those sturdy pedestrians who care not to tramp eight or nine miles to Suffern's, and thus examine the interesting valley we are now leaving.

A few miles beyond Monroe Works, the very crest of the hill-sides are carried by the plow, and the shaven ridge is marked with fences and dotted with trees, converting the heights into the character of Orange county summits. We are now fairly in sight of the "land flowing with milk and *butter*," and the receding hills seem to bow their heads, and sink lovingly in the embrace of the wide fields and pastures stretching flatly before us. Now and then, however, the mountains close up near us, as is the case on approaching the next station, called

TURNER'S (from New York 47 miles, from Dunkirk 413 miles). This is the most important station on the road

 thus far, showing something more than a platform for idlers and milk-kettles. Large freight-houses, and the numerous farm-wagons standing near, show that this is a great converging point for travelers and produce to an important back country. The place was formerly called Centerville, but now is named after the owner of a hotel in the village, in the rear of the station, where are also extensive flour-mills. He is proprietor of the surrounding land, on which there is plenty of game, so that *Turner's* is a favorite resort for a day's sport to our city gentry.

The road now enters a fine rolling country, where the vast pasturages and scant woods show that we are entering the heart of the *dairy region*, that has made Orange county, to house-keepers from Maine to Texas, a synonym with butter and milk; and one of the largest of these depôts we recognize in the next stopping-place, the village of

MONROE (from New York $49\frac{1}{2}$ miles, from Dunkirk $410\frac{1}{2}$ miles). This neat little village, the largest we have reached since leaving Piermont, is said to be the greatest milk depôt on the road, as you may judge from the number of cans waiting for a down trip and those discharged. Two hundred cans are said to be sent hence to New York every day, each can averaging about 15 gallons. The milk is furnished in different lots by adjacent dairy-men, some of whom own from 60 to 90 cows. Dealers in New York contract for this article at two cents per quart, delivered at the depôts. Its freight costs half a cent per quart. The increasing demand for milk increases the value of land, and makes it profitable to the dairyman. The superior quality of the milk of Orange is owing

to the peculiar nature of its grasses, which, with plenty of good water and long skill in dairy farms, puts this county at the head of all pasturages.

A person stopping a day at any of these milk depôts will soon see the keenness of the dairy-men to convert every drop of the staple into gold. Just as the California miner does not deck his person with "big *specimens*"—just as the town of Cologne does not apply its fragrant staple to purify its own foul self—just as a confectioner does not realize a child's belief that he breakfasts upon candy and dines upon *bon-bons,* so the dairy-men of Orange show their indifference to milk and butter as luxuries! They literally do not know "on which side their bread is buttered," because they *use* none, and to their fastidious palates, cream *spoils the flavor of tea!* Those of you, then, that preserve your early love for bread and butter, and believe in the essentiality of cream to a cup of "China's fragrant herb," go not to Orange any more than you would visit Champagne for a draught of choice Sillery! The effect of this love of gain is to decrease the amount of butter made in Orange, the sale of its original form being more lucrative.

Monroe is a thriving village, having several spacious stores, a hotel well kept and comfortable, and contains about 700 inhabitants. It was first settled in 1742, under the name of Smith's Clove. It next figured under the funny title of *Cheese Cocks!* In 1802 it was renamed Smithfield, and at last, in 1808, it was changed to its present patriotic but *universal* title, after President Monroe. It got its first name from its settler, one Claudius Smith, afterward a notorious chief of the "Cow Boys" of the Revolution, who made the country, extending as far as Ramapo, the scene of their murders and depredations. He was hung by the Whigs in 1779, and his son Dick, in revenge, eclipsed his father in infamy. In Eager's History of Orange County, the reader will find an interesting account of these villains, their misdeeds, and the punishment they suffered. No better materials for a romance of the rogue and ruffian school can be found any where. The aforesaid Claudius Smith would make a capital hero. He was well educated, had wit, and a tall, handsome person. Here are two specimens of his waggish humor when in extremity. Just before the hangman "worked him off," a person he had robbed of some valuable papers begged him to reveal where they were. "Wait till you see me in the next world," was the cool reply of Claudius. In his early wicked youth, his mother had predicted he would die "*like a trooper's horse, with his shoes on!*" a prophecy the Cow Boy remembered, and belied by kicking off his shoes as soon as he had mounted the scaffold.

At Monroe we again enter a light descending grade, extending 14 miles.

OXFORD (from New York 52 miles, from Dunkirk 408 miles), three miles beyond Monroe, is a neat, thriving place, situated in a part of the country where the surface is more broken into hill and dale. Looking south from the

station, the very choicest specimen of the Orange county scenery may be had here, combining all the elements of a fine pastoral landscape, the cultivated hills receding in the distance, that is closed up by the conical summit of *Sugar-loaf*. The great charm about an Orange landscape is the fact of its being a grazing region. In summer, of course, it does not wear the rich flush which fields of grain lend the prospect; but then, again, instead of unsightly stubble-fields, we see successive pastures, where the cattle wander undisturbed over their rich velvet meadows. Two miles beyond Oxford the road emerges from this rolling country upon a range of marshy, level fields, extending miles in length and one mile in breadth.

At this point (from New York 54 miles, from Dunkirk 406 miles) the branch rail-road to Newburgh starts from the parent stem, and is 19 miles in length. This beautiful road was built by the New York and Erie Rail-road Company, and forms a part of their road. It was opened formally on the 8th of January, 1850. Since then, all the anticipated advantages it held out are in the way of being realized, that is, bringing the west river counties into rapid connection with the *southern tier*. Its width of track is the same as the main road, and cost about half a million of dollars.

The marshy flat extending between this point of junction and the town of Chester, one mile distant, is called *Gray Court Meadows*, and have evidently been the basin of some great sheet of water. The road crosses these meadows by a long, curved embankment, the *visible* portion of which is the least part of its expense or labor, for, in running the track across, the soil was soft to such a depth as to render it necessary to build the road upon a foundation of huge piles, driven nearly ninety feet into the earth, and six feet apart. A most formidable difficulty was thus overcome, and the bog is passed by a high bridge of an enduring foundation. The track is a considerable height above the meadows, and is filled in solidly with earth. These singular meadows are very fertile, and are principally planted with corn. A more extraordinary product, however, has been found in them. Near Chester, a few years since, was found a very fine specimen of the *Mastodon*, the strange animal whose bones so long puzzled naturalists. Many specimens have been found in Orange county, and in Eager's History the reader will find a highly interesting account of the various discoveries. The first mastodon ever discovered in this country was found near Albany in 1705. The next was in Ohio, in 1739. In 1740, large quantities were found near the Big Bone Lick in Kentucky, and carried to France, where it was called the *Animal of the Ohio*. The next locality richest in these relics is Orange county. The first of these was discovered near Montgomery in 1782. Twelve more were found in that vicinity up to 1845. The finest of these was found seven miles east of Montgomery, and had *all* the bones perfect. It was 33 feet long, and six feet below the surface of a peat formation, that extended several feet below the bones, thus preserving the natural standing position of the animal, as though it had been *mired*. Many are the theories of *how* these monsters met their fate, and we will refer the curious reader to Mr. Eager's compiled explanations, as they will be found very entertaining. As a specimen of the author's mode of treating the subject, hear the following points of difference between the mastodon and elephant: "The elephant's toes are built up compactly under his feet, while the mastodon has long, projecting toes. The spinal process of the latter is also longer, thus giving to his neck more upright action, making him *carry a higher head* than the elephant, and *giving him a gay and comparatively sprightly appearance!*" To those who have not "seen" this lively species of the antediluvian "elephant," the author's hints are quite suggestive of the animal's animated bearing! We will also refer to the same book for a copy of a letter written by Governor Dudley to the Reverend Cotton Mather in 1705, concerning the specimens found near Albany. The governor suspected the bones "to be those of a human being whom the flood alone could wash away," and during which, for a while, he might have "carried his head above the clouds" (of course, like the mastodon, with a "gay and sprightly appearance!"), though at last obliged to "give way!" He also thinks this giant must have been "the product of one of those unequaled matches between heaven and earth, of which he had read in the traditions of the Jewish rabbins." But we will not wade deeper into this subject, for fear of being mired ourselves; and with this notice of the fossil products of Orange (quite as remarkable as the statistics of milk and butter), we will hurry across the meadows to the prettily-situated town of

CHESTER (from New York 55 miles, from Dunkirk 405 miles). This is the largest village we have met going from Piermont, from which it is distant 41 miles, and from its station presents a business-like appearance. The village is divided into two parts, East and West Chester, separated by a high hill, topped with neat dwellings, surrounded by gardens. East Chester, that lies near the station, possesses numerous large store-houses, showing the

amount of business done here The population is about 1500. The view from the station, looking east, affords a fine view of the "*meadows*" we have crossed, and to the

southward the cone of Sugar-loaf Mountain towers up in

bold relief. Chester is another stopping-place for travelers bound for Greenwood Lake, eight miles distant.

At Chester the road passes through the hill above the village by a deep cut, and brings us to the very heart of the county, every inch of soil being mapped out into sheets of smooth-shaven slopes, that look like the oldest part of Old England. The farm-houses look neat and substantial, and, after an interesting run of four miles and a half, we enter the far-famed town of

GOSHEN (from New York $59\frac{1}{2}$ miles, from Dunkirk $400\frac{1}{2}$ miles). This is the first incorporated town we have reached, and, with Newburgh, is the half-shire of the county. It is by fame, if not in point of *fact*, the greatest depôt of milk and butter, its *brand* being known throughout the world. The town is situated in the very center of the county, was settled in 1712, and incorporated in 1809. The approach from the east is very beautiful, as the road reveals a glimpse of the public square, neat churches, and public buildings interspersed with trees. We enter the southern suburbs, and pass through the main business street, at the west end of which is the station. The traveler, stepping back into this spacious street, finds himself at once in the center of a bustling, thriving town—

large hotels, extensive stores, and crowds of country wagons showing the current of business done here. A walk

to the public square will show, too, that the Goshenites have great taste and style in the houses of the quieter portion of the town. The only *dark* feature in the aspect of Goshen is the colony of negroes to be found in its southern and western precincts, and who evidently live in a state of squalor and idleness not to be surpassed in any Southern city. They seem as though *ruled* out of the white circles; the men looking idle and dissipated, and the women filthy and abandoned. Let any one saunter round that locality on some warm day, and the swarms of these creatures visible will prove the truth of what is here said of them.

No community along the Erie Rail-road has been more benefited than Goshen. It has been almost *made* by it, and the same may be said of the whole county. We have already alluded to the beautiful buildings that ornament the public square and its neighborhood. Conspicuous among these are the court-house and the monument, that tells of a story of great tragic interest. As this county was the western boundary of the settlements during the Revolution, its history is full of stirring events, in which the settlers struggled with the Indians and their white allies. The flame of patriotism nowhere burned brighter than in this region. It is said that a portrait of George the Third over the court-house entrance, the morning after the arrival of the news of the first conflict with the British troops, was torn down, never again to reappear. The *monument* refers to a very fatal and interesting story. In 1779, John Brandt, the famous chief of the Six Nations and great ally of the British, destroyed the town of Minisink, ten miles west of Goshen, and slew those who could not escape by flight. Laying waste the farms, he retreated, with immense quantities of stock and other booty, to the main body of his forces on the Delaware. A body of 400 men were at once raised in Orange, and dispatched in pursuit. They overtook the Indians near the mouth of the Lackawaxen; but Brandt, by consummate generalship, *dodged* the New York troops, and getting in their rear, finally surrounded them. A murderous fire from the concealed foe at once threw the militia into confusion; but, getting behind trees, they bravely but vainly tried to beat back the fatal circle of their foes. One half of their number had fallen, the rest took to flight; but thirty only returned to tell the story of defeat. Among the slain were some of the chief citizens of Goshen. In 1822, the bones of the slain were collected and brought to Goshen, where they were buried with honors of the most imposing solemnity, in the presence of at least 12,000 persons, drawn from all parts of the adjacent country. Among those present was a Major Poppino, a survivor of the battle, and then nearly 100 years old.

The wealth of Goshen and its surrounding country is well known. The farmers here can boast of fortunes flowing from the excellent product of what *he* of the "*Knick-*

*erbocker*" pleasantly calls their "*udder*iferous kine!" There is one circumstance that must strike every visitor with surprise. The country carts, wagons, horses, and even cattle, which he sees in the market-space near the station, are by no means of such an appearance as he expects to see in a region of such "fatness" as the land of Goshen. On the contrary, one would suppose he were in the most impoverished district of Maryland, and he looks round in vain for the jolly farmer, the plain but substantial wagon, the sleek, well-tended, sturdy draught-horse, or the plump, well-fed kine! If we saw such animals here, Goshen, the *butter-known*, would indeed be a *can*-nie-looking town!

From Goshen the road runs along almost a level, and brings us fairly into the Valley of the Walkill, that runs through this county and Ulster to empty into the Hudson near Rondout. The soil along the Walkill is generally of a peat formation, making extensive marshy flats, called the *Drowned Lands*, similar to the Gray Court Meadows, and in which the mastodon has been chiefly found.

NEW HAMPTON (from New York 63½ miles, from Dun-

kirk 396½ miles) is our next station. It is four miles beyond Goshen, and stands on the west bank of the Walkill.

It is simply a station, consisting of a large hotel, with a few spacious store-houses; in fact, one of the new places that have started into life by the creation of the rail-road, which passes the river by a strong bridge. A short distance below is an extensive woolen factory, which, however, has seen its best days, and looks somewhat decayed. The view of these mills from the bridge is interesting. Here the light descent of the road ceases, and we move over an ascending grade extending several miles.

MIDDLETOWN (from New York 67 miles, from Dunkirk 393 miles), three miles beyond New Hampton, is the next town in importance to Goshen, which it far surpasses in point of manufactures. It has not the dignity and beauty of the latter, having a habit of smoking from its many factory-pipes which Goshen does not indulge in. It is situated in the midst of a rich, level country, and altogether wears a prosperous look. The most important branch of

business done here is the production of stoves and iron ware at the Orange County Foundery, which is quite an extensive establishment, and supplies the whole county. This place is emphatically the growth of the rail-road, and its rapid increase threatens to eclipse Goshen itself. A hill of gradual ascent runs along to the north of the town, which, with its neat churches and other prominent buildings, looks well from that eminence  The great number

of residences scattered along this height show the taste of the richer class of the community.

Leaving Middletown, we soon find ourselves gradually getting into a more rolling and mountainous tract of country, and a rocky cut, which we pass a few miles further, prove that the pleasant fields and gentle vales we have been passing for the last hour must be exchanged for scenery made up of "*sterner stuff.*"

HOWELL'S (from New York 71 miles, from Dunkirk 389 miles), four miles beyond Middletown, is simply a station, with a small hotel and a store or two. From an embankment which we pass here, there is a remarkable view of the high, cultivated mountain ridge, that gradually becomes bolder and higher, a foretaste of the chain of hills we are soon to meet directly across our path. We are now approaching the verge of Orange county. The richness of the soil, however, remains yet manifest in the cultivation of these same hills closing rapidly around us. We must soon bid adieu to the pastoral features of the Orange landscape, which we see in striking perfection when

passing over the curved embankment four miles beyond Howell's. Looking north lies before us a vast range of cultivated valley, skirted with blue hills in the distance,

and on the left swelling into the great bulk of the *Shawangunk* Mountain, that heaves skyward its shaven sides.

This mountain is of an extraordinary character. There is not one inch of its eastern side and its summit that is not of the highest fertility and cultivation, and more so as you ascend from the valley, while its western face (soon to be revealed to us) is a mass of rock and forest, much of it unfit for cultivation, and remaining in a state of primitive wildness. A short distance from this interesting view we arrive at

OTISVILLE (from New York 75½ miles, from Dunkirk 384½ miles). This is a small village, named after its first settler, Isaac Otis, Esq., now a merchant in New York. It has two hotels, and the dwellings on the hill above the

station make a pretty show from the west. It is an important station, having an engine house, &c.; and then, again, it is the furthest verge of the milk region. The milk-trains start from this point, and, of course, that fact gives additional consequence to the place. We therefore take a last look at the *cans* that have been constantly in our sight thus far. We here find ourselves confronted by the great *Shawangunk* ridge, to pass which was for a long time considered the great obstacle to the progress of the road. A tunnel was first proposed, and was so recommended by a board of engineers, to be 2700 feet in length, with grades of 40 feet to the mile for the curves, and 80 feet for the straight sections. This plan was deemed the best means to overcome the height of the mountains, so much greater on the western side, down which it was necessary to pass to the valley below; but it was found that by making the road descend the western side by an extensive curve running south toward the Delaware River, the difficulty could be surmounted without a tunnel. This was the plan adopted and executed, and nowhere can be found a greater triumph of the engineer's skill.

Leaving Otisville, we ascend a grade of 40 feet to the mile, leading to this great passage of the mountain. At the distance of a mile we come to the point where the first struggle with the barrier occurs. This is a thorough rock-cutting, 50 feet deep and 2500 feet in length. Its prodigious "pass" is intersected twice by a turnpike leading from Goshen to Port Jervis, in the valley westward, which shows the roundabout style of travel made necessary by the old modes of conveyance. Emerging from this great cut, we find ourselves on the summit of the ascent, and the road, curving southwardly, proceeds by a slope of many miles along the mountain's side to the valley below. We now catch a glimpse of the west front of the *Shawangunk*, in all its savage and untamed grandeur. This point is also frequently called Deer-park Gap. The word *Shawangunk* is Indian, and means "*white-rocks*," alluding to the color of the rocks to be seen in its breast to the northeast. A little further on we look  down upon the valley we are approaching—an unbroken sea of forest, with not a solitary hut to humanize the scene. No change could be more sudden and complete than what the prospect has undergone in ten minutes since looking at the east front of the Shawangunk. The ascent of this mountain from Otisville is about two miles in length, and here we see the next specimen of heavy work its pas-

sage has made necessary. This is a heavy embankment, supported by a retaining wall 1000 feet in length and 30 feet high. We are now descending the slope of ten miles before us, and the scenery of the valley below is rapidly improving in interest and cultivation. A smile gradually breaks over the dull cheek of Nature. Farm-houses and meadows relieve the solitude of this valley, to which the *Neversink* River gives its name. One of these views is of remarkable beauty. We perceive on the opposite side of the vale a shining

strip of water curving round a spur of the mountains, with a small village adjacent. It is called Cuddeback. This

is the first glimpse we have of the Delaware and Hudson Canal, extending from Rondout to the coal and iron mines at Carbondale, in Pennsylvania. Cuddeback was settled by the Dutch, and is one of the thriving little communities that have sprung up along that important canal. This part of the valley figures conspicuously in the history of Indian warfare. Eight miles beyond Otisville we come to what is called *Shin Hollow Switch*. Here there is a deep cut through a soft soil three fourths of a mile in length and 30 feet deep. This portion of the road is of the most oppressive loneliness, for the valley is completely shut out of sight, soon, however, to reappear in heightened beauty and interest, after passing the

great rock-cutting just two miles ahead of us. The approach to this last formidable barrier in the descent of the mountain is very fine. We reach it by a high curved embankment, and see on each side of us a steep wall of slate rock 50 feet in height and 2500 feet in length. And now let the traveler place himself on the right side of the train (going westward), to catch the noble prospect prepared for him on emerging from this dark pass. At its very portal the road makes a sudden curve southward, and from the precipitous mountain side, along the edge of which we descend, he beholds the enchanting Valley of Neversink in all its cultivated beauty, its western verge bordered by a chain of mountains, at the foot of which gleams the village of Port Jervis, and its level fields losing themselves far in the south, where rolls the Delaware River; beyond which, again, the town of Milford, Pennsylvania, 12 miles distant, may be seen in the misty horizon. A winding grove of trees runs southward over this fair plain, marking the course of the Neversink. A few rods beyond this "cut," the traveler, looking north, may see another superb view, of an opposite character, the mountains swelling

upward in the grandest forms. We have already alluded to the difference between the eastern and western heights of the *Shawangunk* Mountain, that of the west side being 200 feet more than the opposite front. This has caused a

singular difference in the course of the streams of either valley. The Shawangunk Creek, on the east side, runs north to join the Walkill, a tributary of the Hudson, while the Neversink runs south to join the Delaware. The origin of the name *Neversink* is supposed to refer to the steady volume of its stream, always remaining the same.

The descent of the Shawangunk is nearly ten miles in extent, and offers a succession of pleasing views, though becoming more and more contracted in extent. When the slope ceases, our road again turns to the west, and, crossing the Neversink by a bridge 55 feet high, with a span of 150 feet, brings us in full view of *Port Jervis*, that lies beautifully

at the foot of a range of bold and picturesque mountains. Within a few yards, on our left, we have the first view of the Delaware, flowing through its extensive "flats." That river we are now to trace almost to its source. One mile from the bridge over the Neversink, we stop at

DELAWARE (from New York $88\frac{1}{2}$ miles, from Dunkirk $371\frac{1}{2}$ miles). This important station is situated on a

broad area between the Delaware and the open *plateau* on which the village of Port Jervis stands, some half mile north of the depôt, and the whole appearance of the offices of the company, the engine-houses and other buildings,

conveys a just idea of the extent of the business done here. These have caused many dwellings and spacious stores to spring up around, in rivalry to the village on the hill. Among these the *Delaware Hotel* rears its imposing form, and offers excellent accommodations for a large number of visitors, that find its quarters agreeable enough during a sojourn in this picturesque locality. Ascending the height to the village, we find it nestling close to two magnificent high mountains, whose summits beetle over its dwellings, affording extensive views up and down the valleys of the Neversink and Delaware. Port Jervis is named after Mr. John B. Jervis, engineer of the Delaware and Hudson Canal, and owes its origin and growth to that canal, which here passes through it, and, sweeping round these same mountains, extends up the former river in company with the rail-road.

The business done here is chiefly in coal and lumber, and its prosperity is written in the neat houses, churches, hotels, and stores. A large three-story stone grist-mill stands on the brink of the eminence overlooking the station. A mail route passes through from Ulster county to Milford, Pennsylvania, where the tourist should not fail to take a drive, to see the picturesque Falls of the Sawkill in its vicinity. There is every inducement to stop for weeks at Delaware. There are innumerable drives and trips for the pedestrian in every direction, while to the artist there is every variety of scenery, from the bold rocky peak to the long, level flat, with the clumps of beech and willow along the river shore. The Delaware here shows the dangers that are covered over in the depth and force of its current. In dry weather its bed is almost a mass of stones, but the water-marks and wreck along the edge of its banks prove what a fullness and fury attends its freshets. South of the station it is crossed by a ferry, which, when the river "is up and doing" violence, requires the aid of a guide-rope, rigged across the river in an odd fashion. The curious observer of such peculiarities will also be struck with the odd angular dams stretched across its current at low water, at the apex of which is a rough wooden trough. This is the *eel-trap* of the Delaware, which you will see throughout its whole course above this point. The eels of the Delaware are renowned for their delicious flavor—to those who like a fish of such "questionable shape"—and the Cockney that dotes on the eel-pies of Twickenham will vote the Delaware quite as *eel*egant as old Father Thames! A quarter of a mile south of the Neversink bridge that stream empties into the Delaware, and the narrow strip of land formed by this junction is called Carpenter's *Point*. Here the states of New York, New Jersey, and Pennsylvania all unite, and by putting one leg on the small stone marking the spot, one can describe a pirouette over the soil of those three commonwealths. The tourist is again solicited to ascend the heights overlooking Port Jervis, particularly Point Peter, just above the upper village, and the more picturesque peak that forms so remarkable a feature in the view south of the ferry. A nobler panorama is not often seen.

Delaware forms the termination of what is called the "Eastern Division" of the Erie Rail-road, and certainly no work of this sort presents a more interesting variety of soil, scenery, and local history. Traversing the romantic passes of Rockland and the rich and fertile fields of Orange, it takes its way through some of the oldest portions of the state, and gives us, between Otisville and Delaware, but a foretaste of the entirely new tracts of wild, unknown country we will find it is to open up for the first time farther west. In this section of 13 miles were encountered the first serious, difficult opposition of the soil, as may be seen by stating a few items that may prove interesting. Between these points, 317,000 pounds of powder were used, 210,000 cubic yards of rock excavated, 730,000 yards of earth removed, and 14,000 yards of stone wall built. While Otisville is 875 feet above the level of the sea, Delaware is but 500, and the descent between them is one of 45 feet to the mile. The road as far as Delaware was opened in January, 1848; leaving which place we follow the fine section of the road that stretches from the Neversink bridge due west to the extent of three miles, and pass through a spacious area that affords plenty of level ground for the wants of the company at any time. Going west from Delaware to Deposite, a distance of 88 miles, the road is nearly level, the highest grade being 15 feet to the mile. The canal keeps along on our right, occasionally separated from our path, but again closing up, as if to enter its sluggish boats in a race with our iron steed At the end of two miles we enter a rude and uninteresting region, dotted with an occasional hamlet, and though the mountains on the left bank of the Delaware hug the stream, those on the right

recede, leaving a vast plain, across which the canal suddenly bends, and, as we pass it by a wooden bridge, a quiet Dutch picture is given us of its

boats, its slow-plodding steeds in their dreary promenade, and the neat houses dotting the river's banks. Beyond this, a deep gravel cut brings us again to the Delaware, which we cross by what is

called the "*Saw-mill Rift Bridge*" (from New York 92 miles, from Dunkirk 368 miles), four miles from Delaware. This great structure is 800 feet long; it is built of wood,

supported by arches of 160, 150, and 140 feet span, and rests on piers of solid masonry. Its cost was $75,000.

The view up and down the Delaware from this bridge is interesting, particularly the latter, that shows the bold precipice called the "Glass-house Rocks," on the south

bank. The view up stream shows the canal and rail-road now on opposite sides of the river, with an island in the stream that here pours under the bridge a deep and rapid current. In crossing the Delaware, we not only leave Or-

ange county, but enter the land of Penn. The company wished to confine their road to the New York side of the river, but as they could not control the natural features of the country, nor alter state lines, and the narrow strip of passable ground along that bank being already occupied by the canal, the Legislature of Pennsylvania was applied to for right of way through that state. It was also necessary to obtain permission of the New York Legislature to construct a portion of their road up the Valley of the Delaware River, on the Pennsylvania side, and after much difficulty, encountered through two sessions, the privilege was secured; for which right, and *benefit to that state, Pennsylvania charges the company ten thousand dollars a year!* A fine curve in the bank of the river beyond the bridge shows us a broadside view of that structure, with the rocky heights farther on. and in a few moments we are brought opposite the first of those majestic masses of mountain wall

that overshadow our way for miles to come. This huge wall of rock and foliage towers over the right bank of the Delaware, and at its base winds the *thread-like* Delaware and Hudson *Canal*, the figures of the boatmen, horses, &c., dwindled to insignificant size by contrast with the bulky heights above. A short distance up its side is seen a solitary shanty, with men dwarfed to ants, picking out the scant loose soil among the rocks to patch the canal, for over there such an article is as precious as gold dust. There is a breadth and grandeur in this massive mountain screen exceedingly impressive, and the effect is heightened by the simple strip of rail-road and a grove of trees that form the foreground on our side of the river. We are now entering the wild and lonely scenery of the Delaware, and though a farm-house occasionally relieves the solitary and primeval character of the country, they are rapidly becoming less in number, and we wonder that so short a distance should exist between these uncultivated wilds and the teeming plains of Orange. The main employment and support of the population along the Delaware have been, since its settlement, drawn from its lumber, that is carried by rafts down to Philadelphia and other points below; and so the plow and all its civilizing influences has never been felt here, though the poverty of the soil has been a great obstacle. Consequently, except during the rafting season in spring and autumn, the Delaware appears a desolate stream indeed, with nothing to break its monotonous dullness save the occasional shout of the boatmen, the snort of the locomotive, the "still small" lapse of the river over the eel-trap, or the crack of a rifle, as the "far roll of its departing voice" is lost in the echoing hills!

Eight miles and a half west of Delaware we come to STAIRWAY BROOK (from New York 97 miles, from Dunkirk 363 miles). Does not the name of this station suggest a foaming streamlet tumbling down a rocky staircase into the Delaware? Stretch not your head vainly forth with any such expectation, fellow-traveler! Neither stairway nor streamlet is in sight, and near us we see nothing but a wood-pile and water-tank; but turn your eyes toward the river, and look at that beautiful view—the river in the center, a richly-wooded hill on the right, with the canal curving round its base, a pleasing vista of retreating mountains, and this bold foreground,

where a single stately tree, and a humble shanty with a garden-patch, preserve the nice balance between nature and civilization, that gives the prospect such peculiar beauty after the fatiguing solitariness of the scenes just passed.

The snug houses clustering round the locks of the canal opposite are cheering to our spirits, and we feel disposed to answer back the faint hail of the boatmen. Perhaps we may be excused in an attempt to relieve the tedium of the *unassociated* tract of country lying before us by some reflections upon one of the features of the canal, which has been our constant though distant fellow-traveler for so many miles; we mean the *boy-drivers* of the plodding animals that drag those rival vehicles, a near inspection of whom (the boys) affords such a novel study. Before rail-ways had quite abolished in England the old modes of travel, no problem was more puzzling than "What became of the old *post-boys*"—those venerable tenants of juvenile jackets and corduroys? A similar query is suggested by a familiar study of these young canal-boat drivers; and the pencil of Charles Lamb, so happy in sketching those "innocent dark specks of creation," the chimney-sweeps, can alone do justice to these slowest of American jockeys! Only look at the weather-beaten old-young figure bestriding that horse day after day, night after night, through wet and cold. Caught when so young that his legs *protrude* horizontally, and not *hang*, from the saddle, he remains there a *fixture* for his generally brief career—a sort of *youthful Centaur*—and in a short time the mingled air of martyrdom and meditation stamped upon his visage on his first elevation to office gives way to an expression of blank stolidity, the result of his monotonous duties, while the constant exposure to the elements, and the corrupting intercourse of his older associates, make him, while still a child, old in constitution, morals, and disposition, taking from his young face every sign of boyish hilarity, and stamping there revolting traces of early dissipation of the vilest sort. Look at him as he lounges on that plodding horse, under the blaze of a dog-day sun! How listlessly he sits there, in a sort of *sunstruck* doze—his bloated young cheeks, his puffy eye-lids, and the glaring light nearly concealing his glazed eyes—a thing of hopeless inanition, save when he starts up to vent an imprecation upon his charger, or exchange a blackguard jest with some passing vagabond mounted like himself! No blithe country lad is he, with the exhilarating influence of nature's scenes acting upon young, excitable nerves and pulses! Premature bad brandy and tobacco have burned and shriveled up such sensibilities. What to him is the fair, fresh face of the visible world? Nothing but the blank, dead wall of a tread-mill. Perhaps he does now and then glance sidelong at the shadow of himself and steed, and descant on their own deformity. There is no change to his existence save that brought by the seasons, and the cold winter night-winds, when the canal is *not* frozen, that howl down these dreary gorges, pierce through his mass of dirty woolens, and chill his weakened body with rain, sleet, and snow! Like Mazeppa, inexorably and inextricably bound to his horse, no wonder the feeble current in his motionless limbs succumbs to the blast, either crippling him by its nipping breath or stilling it altogether. Hence these unfortunate slow jockeys are often found in the canal, where they have either slipped while locked in half-frozen sleep or whole-drunken stupidity, or, which is quite as likely, by deliberate design to end their sufferings! This is no overdrawn picture of juvenile misfortune, but based on frequent accounts by those who know these boys and their condition. The confinement of the factory-child seems ease and enjoyment compared with this mock liberty and *exercise* of the canal-boat boy! But what has this to do with our *rail*-road? True; and, begging pardon for such an ill-timed piece of sympathy, we will hurry over the three miles from Stairway Brook to

POND EDDY (from New York 99½ miles, from Dunkirk 360½ miles). The Delaware, at this place making a sudden bend, forms one of those wide, deep basins called

*ponds* by the people here, constituting a remarkable feature in the river; hence the name of this station. Pond Eddy is a celebrated rendezvous for the lumber-men when rafting down the river, and during the season this basin is filled with a fleet of their broad vessels. Its depth is great enough to float a man-of-war, and yet a few hundred yards above or below you may see a figure wading through the river to the eel-traps! One can therefore imagine the force of this *eddy* during the rafting season. Pond Eddy is one of the humanized points on the Delaware, owing to the presence of raftsmen, for whose wants good accommodations are here, and the pretty hamlet round the canal-locks on the opposite side, always a charming object in the scenery of this river.

Beyond Pond Eddy the road assumes with every mile a more important character, while the landscape becomes wilder and more lonely. We run along a straight section, 30 feet above the river, marked off by natural abutments of gray rock and pendent hemlocks, that are old enough to have their evergreen foliage changed to a hoary and rusty hue! The mountain we are skirting seems *sliced* down as deep as 115 feet to make our pathway Two miles further we enter a grander portion of the road. The mountains rise perpendicularly from the river's edge,

and along its breast we run securely, though on the brink of a precipice of 80 feet. A huge walled embankment and culvert in the curve of this section add to its interest. But not till we get four miles from Pond Eddy does the splendid engineering talent displayed in the construction of this road show itself in its consummate daring, *sublimity*, and success. It is a section very like the one just passed, but on a grander scale, showing a straight cut along the mountain side one mile long, and terminating in a beautiful curve, whence the best view of it is to be had.

There it stretches, a gigantic gallery overlooking a sheer precipice of 100 feet above the river, and showing along its narrow edge enormous natural abutments of seamed and riven rock, as though they were placed to support the fearful pathway traversed by the heavy train. One of these natural abutments is depicted in the following page. Perhaps it is well that travelers generally see but little of this causeway from the cars, as its sublime features and the cliffs above might make them feel uncomfortable;

but it is well worth the tourist's while to walk along its terrace, in order to judge of the difficulties overcome in running a road along such a frightful precipice. What adds to its impressive grandeur is the contrast presented by the opposite shore, that rises gently from the river, skirted by a grove of willows, over which shines a calm strip of the canal, bordered by smiling fields and snug dwellings. This contrast is more remarkable in the morning, when a vast shadow covers the dark pines and column-like crags that support the grand corridor just traversed, and the opposite meadows, groves, basin, boats, men, and figures sparkle in the dewy light. The solitary shanty near us, with its scant garden-patch, shows the little ground afforded for a human dwelling on our side of the Delaware. It is said that while surveying this portion of the road, it was frequently necessary to let down the engineers by means of ropes to the positions they wished to attain! To convey some idea of the labor expended upon this great Shohola section, we will state that three miles of it cost $300,000! A sustaining wall in the last mile is 90 feet high, and contains 16,000 yards of stone.

We now abruptly leave the Delaware for a while, and pass through a rock-cutting in the mountain dividing that river from one of its tributaries, Shohola Creek,

which we cross by a wooden bridge 70 feet in height. Coming from the rocky grandeur of the section just passed, it is refreshing to meet the strikingly Swiss-like character of this creek, the banks of which are covered with pointed masses of hemlock and pine. While skirting these groves, we see on our right an extraordinary rock-cutting, a perpendicular wall 50 feet high, the masses of which look as square and regular as chisel of mason could make them. Half a dozen tall burned and branchless hemlocks between us and the ravine of the creek makes a strong and savage contrast with the prevailing pictur-

esqueness of its scenery. But the gem of the views along this romantic stream is from the bridge, looking over its shaded dell below toward the village of Barryville, whose white dwellings shine through the tall evergreens springing from the edge of the creek, that is seen to join the Delaware on the right. We have never seen more beautiful nooks than may be found on this creek, of whose musical Indian name (no doubt very expressive of its singular character) we regret not having heard any translation.

BARRYVILLE (from New York 107 miles, from Dunkirk 353 miles). This station lies a short distance beyond the creek, on a highly elevated point above the Delaware, that here makes a sudden bend a mile from the station, showing on its opposite bank the thriving village of Barryville. Shohola, as this station was formerly called, has but little business at present, though with time it must prove an important one, being so near the large village opposite. Barryville is another of the numerous offsprings of the Delaware and Hudson Canal, that passes through it. Besides the coal business established there by that canal, the immense piles of lumber and numerous saw-mills scattered along the shore below us show how much the great staple of the Delaware has to do with the prosperity of the place. A neat little hotel stands opposite this station, and the tourist, tempted to explore its beautiful creek, will

find here those luxuries (so rare in this region), a clean bed and private room. From Shohola the road appears to descend to the river's side from the great height above the river on which the station is placed. It is still, however, a slightly ascending grade, as you may perceive by its current, the river here (between the Shohola and Lackawaxen above) making a gradual descent. In this vicinity was fought the bloody battle, or, rather, ambuscade, when Brandt and his warriors slaughtered and dispersed the New York militia, as noticed in speaking of Goshen, where a monument was erected to the memory of the slain.

LACKAWAXEN (from New York 111 miles, from Dunkirk 349 miles) is our next station, four miles beyond Shohola, and 23 from Delaware. We have, while approaching it, a fine view of the village, the rail-road bridges over the river of the same name, and the great aqueduct here thrown across the Delaware for the passage of the canal, which has so long been our opposite companion. This aqueduct is supported by an iron wire suspension bridge, and conducts the canal over to the valley of the Lackawaxen, up which it extends to Honesdale, Pennsylvania, and is there connected with the mines at Carbondale by a rail-road. Lackáwaxen stands at the confluence of the river with the Delaware, that is here dammed across under the aqueduct, supplying great water-power to the saw-mills in this thriving place. Its iron trade is also of importance, and altogether the station here must prove eventually an important one. The rail-road traverses the Lackawaxen River and part of its vale by two substantial bridges, which, with the aqueduct, make the distant view of the village very remarkable and interesting. Our prurient curiosity to trace the meaning of Indian names was entirely at fault in its attempt to explain the word Lackawaxen, or *Lackawack*, as it is often called. We were told it meant the "junction of streams," a translation we have heard given to a dozen Indian names of different orthography and sound. Could there have been such a radical difference in the dialects of the Indian tribes?

Being the outlet of the valley along which flows such a tide of trade connected with the mines of the interior, the Delaware, and the Hudson, there is every advantage in favor of the great growth of this village and its station. Beyond Lackawaxen we cross a small bridge, and continue following the Delaware, with its rafts, piles of timber, and constant lanes in the mountain's side for the descent of the logs. Further on we leave the river, and five and a half miles from our last stopping-place we reach

MAST HOPE (from New York 116 miles, from Dunkirk 344 miles). This is a station of but little importance, lying in a more open part of the Delaware Valley. Its

name sounds very odd, and is said to be a corruption of two Indian words, whose signification we could not discover.

Two miles further we recross the Delaware into New York by a wooden bridge 580 feet long, with four spans, the two central of which are 160 feet in width. We are

now in Sullivan county, which lies to the west of Orange. This part is called *Lumberland*, though, indeed, that title might be applied to all its southern or river boundary, for there is little but of the soil improved. This part of the county, before the construction of the road, was but little known. The scenery along the river is sensibly becoming tamer than it appears east of Shohola. The road, for four miles beyond the bridge, winds so much that one's ideas of the points of the compass are all at fault, so that, though our general course should be west, we enter Narrowsburgh from the southwest.

NARROWSBURGH (from New York 122 miles, from Dunkirk 338 miles), though not the most picturesque, is cer-

tainly one of the most delightful stations along the road. There is an air of industry, prosperity, and comfort about every thing refreshing to behold after what we have passed. The company's offices are well built, the refreshment-rooms filled with abundance, and near them is a large hotel, kept by Mr. Field, one of the best and most comfortable houses to be found any where. The proof of that is the number of families and single persons that board here during the summer. Narrowsburgh is another of the rapidly-growing communities which the rail-road has scattered along its path. Where, a few years since, were only a farm-house and hotel, now stands a village, with stores and dwellings clustering round the beneficent presence of a *station*. The village, as it may be called, lies on the margin of the Delaware, that here is locked in between

two points of rock, whose narrow gorge gives the place its title of *Narrow*burgh, though the lumbermen call it by its old name, *Big Eddy*, because, during a freshet, there rushes through these "narrows" the "biggest kind" of an eddy. Over the "narrows" is flung a wooden bridge, with a single span of 184 feet—a monstrous span, but not

more so than the monstrous *tolls* for traversing it. These are very high, and act prejudicially to Narrowsburgh, by diverting into other routes the produce that would flow into this station. The amount of business done here is proved by the appearance of the freight-houses. The surrounding country is the region of *tanneries*, owing to the abundance of hemlock; and, in addition to the *leather* interests, the direct communication with the mines of Carbondale supply other sources of trade. The scenery around Narrowsburgh is very beautiful, and affords fine drives and strolling-grounds. The land, fortunately, is in the hands of a gentleman (Mr. Corwin) who has had the good taste to preserve the fine park-like trees dotting the beautiful meadow between the station and the river, and do every thing to make Narrowsburgh a favorite summer resort. Below the narrows spoken of the Delaware expands into a wide basin, which, during a freshet, exhibits a stirring scene. It is said the fury of the current through the "narrows" is such that no boat could live in it; and when large trees heave and toss in its eddies, a wilder scene can not be imagined. Mr. Corwin says he has dropped in it a line 120 feet long, with a weight of 28 pounds attached, *without touching bottom*. In the winter of 1850, when the river was frozen over, a sudden rise of its waters produced a novel scene in that gorge. The pressure of the swollen tide underneath caused the sheet of ice covering the basin below to heave in regular waves, till at last, giving way, the crash and roar of the floating fragments, as they were piled on each other, made a picture of true sublimity.

Another recommendation to a sojourn at Narrowsburgh is the abundance of game. In short, the tourist, artist, and sportsman will find in Mr. Field's hotel the comforts of his own home, and the society of a gentleman ready to impart much information about this very interesting region.

Beyond Narrowsburgh the country reassumes a dull, uncultivated aspect, and one would suppose that the *right of way* through such a district could not be expensive, though, indeed, the poverty of the soil and general worthlessness of a tract are no proofs of the ease with which a road is run through such land. And what a chapter of fun and fury might be found in the *legal* history of a road, growing out of this same delicate question of *right of way*. What sudden rises in the value of gravelly hills or boggy flats occur as soon as such choice territories are threatened with destruction by the appearance of the rail-road! Proprietors, quite willing a few days before to give away every other acre of their darling bogs and gravel-banks, suddenly become afraid of selling them too cheap, and ask the prices of San Francisco town lots! They ask thousands and get hundreds; and though their sales make them comfortable for life, many remain sworn enemies to the very road that enriches them! If the land agents of the company would only publish their diaries, they would excel in fun just as the Diary of a Physician does in tragic interest. And while on the subject of the right of way, listen, fellow-traveler, to this odd illustration of it that occurred during the first survey of the road, near Monroe. While the engineers were running a line in that quarter, one of these *land*ed gentry refused them permission to effect their purpose through a certain field of his. They did not notice his warning or his threats; but one morning, just as they had assembled with their tools on the forbidden ground, a ferocious bull rushed upon them, roaring like one of his Bashan progenitors, with tail erect and head lowered in a very threatening manner. The farmer had placed him there in ambush the night before, and now stood near, watching the issue of the conflict. A very short *survey*, indeed, of the animal, was needed by the engineers, who forthwith "*ran a line*" to the fence with unexampled directness and dispatch. The bull, thus left master of the field, amused himself with a stampede among the deserted instruments. A parley was then held, and the professionals declared that if the bull was not removed they would shoot him; and some shooting-irons being soon produced for that purpose, the farmer gave in, and the bull was taken out. It seemed, however, that the animal "fed fat the ancient grudge" he bore the profession, for when the first locomotive appeared on the scene of his defeat, he lay in ambuscade for the unconscious engine, and, rushing toward it, they met in full career, and his bullship was converted into fresh beef on the spot!

Four miles beyond Narrowsburgh the monotonous and solitary track along the river suddenly emerges into extensive plains of the greatest fertility. Orchards are interspersed among these, and, two miles of these cheering fields being passed, we stop at

COCHECTON (from New York 131 miles, from Dunkirk 329 miles). The station here is of the simplest description; but the views from it, looking toward the village and up and down the valley, are truly beautiful (see next page). The valley of the Cochecton presents the richest *streak of fat* mercifully inserted between the two solitary and barren banks of this lumbering river. It is about two miles long, averaging one mile in breadth. One mile from the station we enter the valley, and, while the Delaware

keeps close to the mountains to the west, the rail-road follows the curving base of the hills on the east, thus mak-

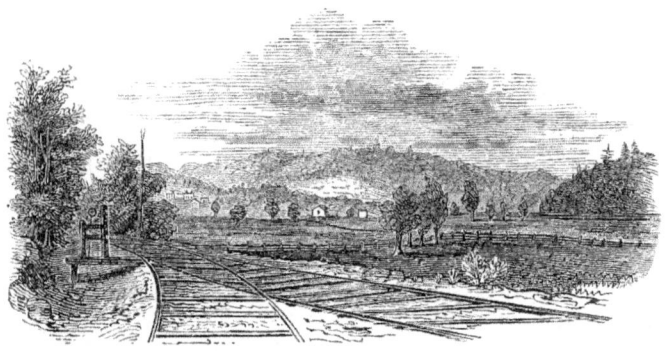

ing the valley elliptical in form, for at the distance of two miles road and river again unite. The valley is evidently an alluvial deposite, as hardly a stone can be found upon its level surface, while fifteen feet below are found cobble-stones precisely like those forming the bed of the river. At the southern end layers of leaves have been found several feet under ground, well preserved, and lying in a strata of sand and earth. This character of the soil throws an air of probability over the correctness of the signification given to the name of the valley—Cochecton—which is said by the inhabitants to mean "increase," and by the Indians used to describe the formation of its soil. In the spring of the year, the waters of the Delaware above Narrowsburgh are, during freshets, sometimes so dammed up by the narrow gorge they pass through at that place, that this valley is quite inundated. The sediment thus deposited enriches the land to its present fertility, and crops of rye, oats, buckwheat, and corn are very productive. Along its rich acres are some twenty dwellings, two churches, and two stores. The Newburgh turnpike crosses the valley mid-length, and passes over the Delaware by a wooden bridge. On the other side of the river at that point lies the town of Damascus, a thriving Pennsylvania community, finely situated in a beautiful glen, that furnishes water-power for the mills of the village. A large academy has just been erected there. The country around Damascus abounds with scriptural names, and furnishes in this respect an odd contrast to this section of the New York branch of the Delaware, where the musical and expressive names used by the Indians are carefully preserved. It is amusing to hear the honest denizens of this region speak of the change caused by improved means of travel. Many of the old settlers here still remember when Newburgh was the nearest market, and that over rough roads, involving a journey of days; now six hours only are sufficient to bring them to the greatest of all markets, New York city, a distance of 122 miles. Beyond Cochecton the road rejoins the river, and for some dozen miles follows the windings of its stream through scenery which, neither wild nor stupid, becomes positively tiresome from its sameness and tameness. There are few traces of man in these tracts, and when the river is low a torpor seems to rest over the succession of sleek, sloping points of its shores, that shows nothing but a solitary raft half aground, or a faint attempt at a smile from the ripple over the eel-dam. Not even the fact that this was the scene of the stirring incidents in Cooper's "Last of the Mohicans" lights up the scenery with interest, and we rejoice when, at the end of four miles from Cochecton, we see the round slopes of the mountains breaking up into rugged profiles, and a rock-cutting or two threatening to topple down upon us. Six miles beyond Cochecton we cross the Calicoon Creek by a wooden bridge, and reach the station of the same name.

CALICOON (from New York 136 miles, from Dunkirk 324 miles) stands in the heart of a wild, and, till lately, unknown country. Not many years since wild animals roamed the forests along its creek, and a race of old hunters dwells here, that still recount their adventures with them and the Indians. Tanneries now abound in the neighborhood, and the leather and other freight in the store-houses prove that, lonely as the station appears, its business is not slight. The Calicoon Creek is full of wild scenery, and is stocked with game and trout. Its name —*Calicoon*—has caused a war of opinion among the inhabitants on its banks. Some say it is the Indian word for *turkey*, a bird that once abounded here, and gave the stream its name. Others insist that it is of Dutch origin, and also means *turkey*. Our informant inclines to the first theory, and bases his belief on the authority of one Tom Quick, of whom he tells the following little story, illustrative of the habits of the Indian fighters of this region. *Bill Quick*, the father of Tom, was one of the most noted of these hunters and fighters. The

Indians murdered Bill's father, and the son swore revenge upon them to the extent of *one hundred lives*, that being his sire's estimated value in red-skins. Bill hastened to put his vow in execution, and no amateur dog-slayer in the month of August ever went to work with more zeal than did Bill with his knife and rifle. Those trusty weapons every day gave him his daily head. He did not carry off their *scalps;* those would have been but common-place certificates of his performances. He brought away their entire heads, and, having dissected and labeled them, carefully put them away on shelves in his hut. The collection of heads thus "wisely kept for show" rapidly increased with his skill and practice. His vigilance was as extraordinary in eluding his foes as in decapitating them. In vain they tried to entrap the pale face whom they knew was thus rapidly thinning out their tribe. At last the mortality became so great, and his safety seemed so secure, that they, believing him to use supernatural agency, avoided him and his haunts altogether. This did not please the collector of Indian heads, for, his *returns* beginning to come in more slow, he feared that too many years would be necessary to accomplish his vow. His skulls now increased slowly, though steadily, and an acute chronologist might have guessed the increasing lapses of time between the red "flesh-tints" of his last deposite and the mellow hues and ivory gloss of its predecessor. Time, too, was doing his work upon Bill. The eye of the bold hunter of men was growing less keen in detecting the redskins, his step not so active in dodging them, and his hand shook while "covering" them with his rifle. Age, however, could not quench his determination to fulfill his vow. However languidly he awoke in the morning, one glance at the shelves of his grinning phrenological cabinet would make him bounce out of bed, seize his rifle, and take to the woods. In this pious work the hunter grew old. His son *Tom*, long since a man grown, had often wished "to follow to the field his warlike lord," "but his sire denied." Bill would allow no partnership, and resolved to finish the bloody game as he commenced it, *single-handed*. At last the *ninety-ninth* Indian skull was deposited with the others, and Bill, pleased at the thought of soon wiping out the "*to be continued*" he had chalked upon the last of his collection, prepared for his last sortie, quite willing, if it proved successful, for his own bones to be "laid on the shelf!" It might have been the agitation caused by this thought of a speedy fulfillment of his vow that made old Bill suddenly ill, and then he knew his time had come. Calling his son Tom to his bedside, he told him he was dying, and that he had a legacy to leave him. "That row of Injun skulls, Tom! There's ninety-nine on 'em, and I swore to make 'em a hundred, but the Lord won't let me, Tom, but wants you to finish the job! I charge you to do it, Tom, or your father's ghost, and your murdered grandfather's too, will come and haunt you!" With this exhortation, the old hunter, with his eyes fixed on his trophies, gave up the ghost.

Now whether old Bill had drove off the Indians, or made them too cautious, or Tom was unskillful, does not appear, but the son did not prove equal to the task solemnly imposed upon him. In vain did Tom scour the woods, and try his best to catch the "last of the Mohicans." Years rolled past, and the niche on the shelves still remained vacant. The effect of his failures were disastrous upon Tom. He lost all confidence in his abilities, and sank into fatalism. "It was *jest* his luck!" With a son's pride, he would survey his hereditary skulls, and sigh for the glory of adding to them the last skull, at that time so provokingly safe upon its proprietor's shoulders! From these interviews between the "quick and the dead" he would retire, downcast and despairing, and finally sought relief for his troubled conscience in the "last infirmity of noble minds"—the bottle! "How could he get the hundredth head, when there were no Injuns to grow 'em?" And then Tom drank a bumper to the rest of the soul of his grandsire, whom he thought ought to be content with the not very "vulgar fraction" of ninety-nine Indian lives. Amid these potations, however, would appear the figure of his father wrapped in bear-skin—"his habit as he lived" —who, pointing to the incomplete row of heads, would shake his fist at Tom; and then the skulls would grin, and skeleton thumbs would appear at their snubby skeleton noses, and skeleton fingers would wag their rattling joints at him; and then his father's ghost would chant forth old *hundred*, and Tom would rush out, staggering, with his rifle, to return empty-handed, as usual. In this way Tom has lived to be an old man, his energies wasted and his health impaired by the heavy thought of the non-execution of his father's dying request. Like Hamlet, he is the victim of a false position—unequal, though inclined to accomplish the mission imposed upon him. With the "sweet prince," he might rail against the "cursed spite" of being born to reduce the dislocated joints of his sire's soul, and paraphrase his invective thus:

"Injuns are out of date! Oh, cursed blunder,
That I was born to make these skulls *a hunder!*"

HANKIN'S (from New York 143 miles, from Dunkirk 317 miles), seven miles beyond Calicoon, where we next stop,

is another secluded station, standing in a level plain midway across a bend in the Delaware. The business done here, though, will undoubtedly increase. Half a mile this side of Hankin's the road runs along the base of a mountain, whose steep sides are swept entirely bare of trees, presenting nothing but a mass of stumps and rocks, where the rattle-snake is found in myriads. This removal of the forest was the few minutes' work of a hurricane twenty years ago; and it is a pity that the same shaving process has not been extended to more of these bold peaks, for it is refreshing to turn from the eternal green mounds skirting our rivers to such a bluff, bald veteran as this fellow, that flings his rocky outlines athwart the sky as though proud of his distinction above the common herd.

We rejoin the Delaware at another of its numerous rafting stations. These signs of the lumber business are an indispensable feature in the Delaware landscape. Even when it is not the season for rafting, you will see these light, broad craft moored along the banks, or, like huge crocodiles, sprawled upon the beach. Those of dressed

timber are neatly put together, and are of various sizes, some long enough to stretch across the river at some places. The logs of hemlock that form the other rafts are slid down from the steep sides of the hills, that show narrow lanes, along which, and at the bottom on the waterside, you may see the barkless timber glistening in the sun—another peculiar feature in the landscape of this river. When the formation of the ground does not permit this expeditious mode of sending down the logs, the patient ox team is seen on the shore, dragging them to where the raftsmen can put them together. It is a pretty scene when such a group is seen hard at work, the sturdy lumbermen half immersed in the stream, or mounted on the timber in various attitudes of collecting or steering them. No picture of this river can be a portrait without these characteristics.

Passing along the winding river, the next object of interest is a slight thread of a cascade, that tumbles over a precipitous mountain 500 feet in height, coming down to the very edge of the road. It is seven miles beyond Hankin's; but you need not look out for it unless the clouds have supplied it with water, for in dry weather there is nothing of the kind visible at all. During a wet day in winter it spouts in admirable profusion, for then the dense foliage screen of summer no longer hides its successive leaps from cliff to cliff. We have now passed from Sullivan county into Delaware, one far superior in every respect. The portion of the road traversed since leaving Lackawaxen is of an almost level grade, and presenting but few marks of heavy work in its construction. Keeping generally near the edge of the river bed, but little elevated above it, it occasionally presents a rock-cutting on one side and a sustaining wall on the other; but these, after having seen the great three-mile cut near Shohola, excite no interest.

EQUINUNK (from New York $153\frac{1}{2}$ miles, from Dunkirk $306\frac{1}{2}$ miles) we next reach, 10 miles beyond Hankin's, another young but growing station, the product of the road. At present it consists of the company's offices and

a neat hotel, that will do much to hasten the growth of a place promising to become an important depôt, for there is a vast region, both on the Pennsylvania and New York sides of the river, that must become tributary to it. It takes its name from the village of Equinunk, in Pennsylvania, seen on the river side, glimmering at the foot of that conical mountain, one mile to the southward. The traveler will be struck with the beauty of that village, as we approach it by the curved embankment on our side of

the river. Equinunk village is placed in the region of tanneries, and possesses several that support its population. Until the erection of the hotel at the station, visitors had to seek accommodation in the village. A bridge over the Delaware at this point, it is thought, would act beneficially upon the business of the station. If the traveler first sees Equinunk village at sunset, he will find it one of the prettiest views on the Delaware. The neat dwellings and mills are brilliantly relieved against the valley, shaded by the noble mountain swelling above the village on the right, while a bold precipice of gray rocks reflect a broad blaze of light on the left. These sparkling objects, together with the ferryman slowly pulling over the stream, are vividly repeated in the Delaware, here of great depth and transparency.

STOCKPORT (from New York $159\frac{1}{4}$ miles, from Dunkirk $300\frac{3}{4}$ miles) is our next stopping-place, four miles further, and also takes its name from a busy little community on the Quaker side of the river. The business of this station is on the same scale and of the same character with that of Equinunk. The village opposite was named after a

town in England, and has a large grist and saw-mill, the property of Mr. ———, whose grandfather settled this place. The immense piles of sawn timber and logs collected here attest its importance as a lumber depôt; and, like Equinunk, it is placed in a very lovely bend of the river. Stockport is the last place of importance we shall see on the Delaware proper, for we now approach the point when the stream we have so long followed loses its one and indivisible name, and divides into two branches. It is evidently shrinking in size, though occasionally expanding to great but shallow width; the islands of soft soil, covered with bushes, which we first met near Equinunk, are now imposing tracts of pasture, with large picturesque trees with exposed roots, entangled with mossy wreck, making it look more like the lovely Susquehanna than the monotonous and shore-washed Delaware. The traveler should keep on the left side of the cars if he wishes to enjoy the beautiful view where the two branches unite to form this river. The exact point of confluence is not visible, but the view near it is very interesting. Three miles beyond Stockport this meeting of the waters takes place. Before you, on the left, comes their united current, flowing through a wide flat flanked by gravelly points, clumped with noble trees. A range of mountains is seen on either side, but the peculiar feature in the view is the conical peak of the mountain filling up its center,

with its base mapped off into meadows, and its upper half an unbroken forest. This picture should be first seen at sunset, when the purple mass of the mountains is reflected in the river, save where its shallow bed breaks it into a bright ripple, across which you may often see the darkened figures of damsels *wading*. That is a custom much honored in this region when the Delaware is low; and it is a piquant sight to witness their dainty style of fording, indulging in many a "graceful bend" as their tender soles come in contact with envious gravel; or, suddenly plumping into unexpected depths, they regulate with modest ingenuity the height of their garments above the enamored tide! From this point we leave the river suddenly, passing through a fine plain of great fertility; we then cross the east branch of the Delaware by a long wooden bridge, and find ourselves in that most beautiful of all villages along the road,

CHEHOCTON (from New York 164 miles, from Dunkirk 296 miles). Thanks to the resolute taste of those who

retain the expressive and musical Indian name of this romantic spot !* The name of *Hancock* is given to the township, and some persons will apply it to Chehocton; which, however, is undergoing corruptions enough, such as *Shehocking*, and, shocking to say, *Shocking* itself. Chehocton means the "union of streams," and is well applied to the meeting of the east and west branches of the Delaware, whose Indian names are Popacton and Coquago. These streams both rise in the northeast, and run southwest, almost parallel, for nearly 70 miles. At that point the largest or west branch (Coquago) is suddenly turned from its course by the ridge separating this valley from that of the Susquehanna, and runs southeast about 13 miles to Chehocton. The Popacton, or east branch, leads a much shorter but more consistent career, keeping due on in the direction (southwest) to meet its ally. These two streams, rushing toward each other, are about to unite at Chehocton, when, in the felicitous words of Mr. Willis, "lo! a mountain puts down its immovable foot, and forbids the union!" Chehocton stands upon the

---

* These thanks are now, alas! undeserved, the village being decidedly dubbed Hancock since this book was written.

narrow neck of land, only half a mile wide, separating the streams, that again turn southward, and finally meet two miles below, at the southern point of the conical mountain we saw there, and whose northern spur is thrust forward to "forbid the union." Chehocton extends from this point eastwardly to the bridge over the Popacton; and a view of it from any of the adjacent heights will convince any one that a more beautifully situated village is to be found in no country. The view we give is from the west, showing how snugly the village is lapped among

the mountains, beneath the farthest of which is seen the approach by rail-way from the east by the bridge over the Popacton. The view from the north, looking down the Delaware, is the most extensive, however, and is unequaled along the river.

Chehocton is the most important station reached since leaving Delaware, and its growth is amazing. Before the road was extended here it was a dull post-town, and, though on the main road from Delhi to the Pennsylvania mines, presented nothing of the activity and increase now visible in every part of its romantic locality. Two large hotels and several extensive stores now ornament its street, which, with the spacious buildings of the station, give it an air of importance and dignity. Private dwellings, inclosed with gardens, embellish this thoroughfare, while the stores look neat, but rather grand, from behind their Corinthian piazzas, particularly when the eye turns from these classic temples to the humble house of God conspicuously placed among them, and which should at least be newly painted and have a paling around it. Some shrubbery, also, would make it really the ornament to the village, which a distant view of its modest little spire suggests it must be. Chehocton is destined to be an important place. With a rich back country, its business has been much increased by new facilities for bringing here the tributary produce and trade that once diverged to more accessible points, like Deposite. This has been effected by a new *plank road*, extending in the interior to *Walton*, in Delaware county. Besides these advantages, its natural attractions, pure air, and romantic scenery must soon cause the gentle heights above the village to be covered with country seats. In the mean time, let the tourist, artist, and sportsman visit it, and they will find its attractions doubly pleasant while enjoying the excellent accommodations of the hotel kept by Mr. Faulkner. There is a saline spring on the Popacton, which a medical gentleman assures us has valuable medicinal qualities. The population of Chehocton is about 800. It is remarkable, on looking over a gazetteer of but five years back, to see how briefly are noticed, or, rather, not noticed at all, many of the now thriving places along this rail-road. Chehocton is one of these villages that have outgrown such recent records, and had important confessions to make to the census-takers of 1850. We leave this beautiful village by a deep cut through the sloping ridge of the mountain that "forbids the union" of the Delaware's branches, and in a few minutes we come in view of the Coquago, or west fork, which, for three miles, we follow close along its bank, and find it, for that distance, beautiful enough, but certainly not deserving the flattering title of "the Rhine of America," bestowed by Mr. Willis. We

think it far inferior, in every respect, to the east branch, and beyond the distance specified it becomes positively stupid. Some miles further the road passes, by a very long, straight section, through a fertile plain; and then, crossing

the Coquago by a covered wooden bridge, we roll along a curved embankment, that brings us to

DEPOSIT (from New York 177 miles, from Dunkirk 283

miles). This is an important station: it is 13½ miles from Chehocton — 162½ from Piermont: it is the terminus of the long, gentle grade extending over the *Delaware Division* from Delaware sta-

tion, and the starting-point of a heavy grade that leads to the passage of the high mountain ridge between us and the Susquehanna. The station is at the west end of the village, that extends eastward, abreast of the embanked approach, as far as the Coquago, which we leave at the bridge just crossed, bidding a final adieu to this last scion of our old companion, the Delaware. The eastern portion of Deposit is the oldest, and, till lately, the busiest; but now, in spite of its numerous old hotels, churches, mills, bridges, and dwellings, the bustling precincts of the sta-

tion, its large, new, and improved hotel, and the rows of dashing, spruce stores, with Corinthian fronts, have altogether made the west end of Deposit, as of all other communities, *the* place of business. A plank road intersects the road at this place from Bainbridge, Chenango county. A glance at the freight-houses and offices of the company shows the amount of business done, and the numerous tracks and switches laid down in the broad area of the station indicate what is expected to be its increase. Unlike Chehocton, there is no beauty in its situation to arrest the traveler beyond one of the most abundant refreshment-tables a hungry tourist ever looked at. The important character of the road over the mountain's barriers ahead of us makes this station particularly extensive in its force of trains and engines. An excellent new hotel is conveniently near the offices. Tanning is carried on here to an immense extent, a constant exchange being kept up with New York by returning the dressed hide for the raw material. The population of Deposit is about 1200.

In leaving Deposit, we pass out of Delaware county and enter that of Broome. The one we leave has about one fourth of its surface under cultivation, though the soil is generally good and the valleys very fertile. The introduction of the rail-road, however, will develop its agricultural resources and make them flourish, just as its lumbering interests have done by reason of the easy outlet furnished by water communication.

A run through a straight section of one mile due west from Deposit brings us to Oquago Creek. This is the last tributary of the Delaware we meet, whose waters we have now traced through a distance of 90 miles. Here ends the slight ascending grade extending from Delaware, and here, too, begins the grade of 58 feet per mile we must ascend to surmount the high mountain wall between us and the Susquehanna. The summit we are to cross is 1366 feet above the level of the sea, and Deposit is only 997—a difference to be overcome in about eight miles. Passing the Oquago and two heavy rock-cuttings, reminding us of Shohola, we now begin our sidelong ascent of the mountain. Every rod of it attests the labor here encountered, and the scenery suddenly assumes all the wild, blighted features to be found wherever these severe struggles with the ground occur. The rocky rubbish, the scattered, splintered, and burned trees in every possible posi-

tion, show the first obstinate resistance made to the engineer, and a lonely shanty, half buried in the riven earth, only adds to the desolation of the battle-ground. The whole ascent is full of interest. Spur after spur of the mountain is doubled in our upward, spiral flight, and every curve in the road presents new views of savage landscape. The wildest of these you may see four miles from Deposit, where we reach an extensive gravel bank. Ap-

proaching this at sunset, the laborers look like ants busily at work, while the huge bonfires made of the tree-stumps, the hemlock groves, the yellow bank, and figures of the workmen, form a picture worthy of "Savage Rosa."

A little beyond this there are some superb views up and down the valley on our right, while we cut our way along

the mountain side by means of prodigious embankments. Within two miles of the top, the few houses occasionally seen on our right entirely disappear, and we enter a perfect solitude—a close forest of somber hemlock, whose blackened stems, and broken and scattered trunks are in fit keep-

ing with its oppressive gloom and silence (see cut at head of next page). Glad to escape from this dismal avenue into a sunny clearing, we soon enter a straight cut of a mile running west, and there, "darkly painted on the crimson sky," stands the enormous portal through the mountain top that fitly gives its name to the station of

SUMMIT (from New York 184½ miles, from Dunkirk 275½ miles). In approaching this prodigious pass, the traveler

should bribe the engineer for the privilege of one of his windows, and see it as we describe it at sunset. From the ordinary seat of a car you can see nothing of its irregular profile, as it looms up before a black mass of rocky outline, having no foliage of any sort to soften its severe features, and only crested with half a dozen branchless

hemlocks, some 80 feet in height, bristling on the right edge of the gap, serving us to judge of the height of the cut, which, from its top to the track, is 200 feet. The left side is a sheer precipice nearly, but the profile of the right bank is finely broken up, showing first a mass of slate rock 60 feet high, and then, sloping upward with loose, crumbling stone, it terminates in a crest of splintered rock, tipped with the blighted hemlocks. One of these trees reclines over the ledge in a very curious and imminent way, as though it would every moment dart downward. Between you and this pass is a *table-land* on each side of the track, covered with shanties and half a dozen wretched houses, of the tenants of which you are not long kept in doubt by the rich brogue issuing from them. A simple platform constitutes the station here— quite sufficient for its wants, as one may judge on looking over the wild and unimproved settlement adjoining. It is well worth while for the traveler to ascend the right cliff of the "cut." The view westward from that point is extraordinary, and in winter presents the very picture of extreme desolation, when the shanty roofs are but just

above the snow, and the scorched and *charred* hemlocks and black rock of the pass look doubly black, looming out from the mantle that whitens all things else. Such a mass of riven rock, and of burned, fallen timber, never were huddled together as you see here on this pinnacle, swept clean by the tempests. The last desperate stand against the engineer was made here; and the charred fragments of bulky trees look as though vanquished Nature had here sought her funeral pyre!

There is a large water-tank at the mouth of the cut, and a "*turn-out*," with engine-house, in case an engine may be required at this point. The accumulation of snow in the jaws of the *cut* often arrests the progress of the train, and then extra locomotives are ordered up from Deposite or from Susquehanna, on the other side of the summit. It puzzles one to know what supports the tenants of those shanties of a kennel's size and a pig-sty's cleanliness; but they are occupied by workmen engaged along the road in this region, who found convenient these huts, established at the "summit" during the long siege of its rocky barrier. Oh, Ireland! if your sons would only apply a little of their irresistible *pioneer* muscle, that has so universally *cleared* the earth of its obstacles to civilization, to the task of *beautifying* the soil thus prepared, what a garden this western world would be. But no! though this little bit of level soil under the shadow of the *summit* is not ungrateful, the denizens of those styes scorn the "*foreign* aid of ornament" or tidiness; and so that puddle is found to be convenient near the door, and that barrel makes a good chimney, and flowers don't support life, and so the pigs walk in and out as they please.

The *cut* through the summit winds along half a mile, though it does not retain its rocky character far beyond the eastern entrance. It is not delved through a continuous or compact mass of rock, but in many parts the sides are of a soft, crumbling texture, which, by the constant dripping from the solid ledges, are turned into a sort of paste on each side of the road. The geological student will find

this a great field of study. These drippings during winter form enormous icicles, hanging like pointed gray-beards from the rugged cheek of the pass, and falling in fragments below by the concussion of a passing train. We have stood in that pass during the hottest days of the year, and found the air cool; and in the winter old Boreas howls along its corridor as though it were a musical hall expressly made for the exercise of his lungs. The cost of this rock-cut through Summit was over $200,000.

Leaving this magnificent monument of the enterprise of the company and the skill of the engineer, we now descend the mountain by a grade of 60 feet, and nearly of the same length with the eastern ascent. We are entering the picturesque portion of the road, or what is called by the profession the "Susquehanna Division." Who that was one of the party will ever forget the first memorable crossing of the mountain, in December, 1848, when the road was formally opened from Delaware as far as Binghamton; and when the elements conspired, but in vain, to keep back the festival trains, that cut their way through the snow. The crossing of the Alps by Napoleon's legions was not more glorious or wonderful; and the acclamation of the people that waited our arrival along the track, in the midst of the most violent of snow-storms, proved how welcome were these conquerors of space, and harbingers of trade, intercourse, and civilization.

Four miles of the descent from *Summit* are as stupid as can possibly be. The view is shut in by the wood on each side, and not even a shanty peeps out from its dull covert. But this same section acts as a whet to our keen curiosity for what is beyond; and it is first gratified by our arrival at the famous

CASCADE BRIDGE (from New York $188\frac{1}{2}$ miles, from Dunkirk $271\frac{1}{2}$ miles). This stupendous wooden structure consists of a single arch, 250 feet in width, thrown over a ravine 184 feet in depth. The span of the arch has a rise of 50 feet, and we believe far surpasses in width any other in the world constructed of timber. This ravine is very narrow, and is approached and crossed so rapidly that a person in the cars  can form no idea of the bridge itself, though we can see the gulf, and judge of its depth by a glance at the *tops* of the pines, descending, row by row, to the rocky, thread-like stream at the bottom of its gloomy jaws. To judge of the bridge and the gulf properly, it must be explored leisurely, and a day can easily be consumed in examining both from their various points of view. Descending the east side by a path supplied with a secure balustrade in the shape of stout saplings, we come to the bottom of the gulf, and see this wonderful structure, as it were, suspended in the air above us, so airily, with all its strength, seems its graceful arch to span the chasm. The train crossing it now looks like a toy-cart, and the laborers at work on the west side are dwindled to mere atoms. Following up the stream, we stand immediately under its

arch, and can well see the huge ribs, joints, and sinews that form its powerful anatomy. This is the best point of view whence to comprehend the strength and beauty of the work. Instead of resting upon frail piers erected by the hand of man, each leg of the arch is supported on and in deep *shelves* hewn into the solid rock, that rises wall-like on both sides of the chasm; and while these eternal foundations stand, so will the bridge. Its arch is made of eight ribs of white oak, two feet square in the center, and two feet by four at the abutments. These are interlaced with wood and iron braces in a way to show how well strength is combined with lightness in its airy structure. The width of the bridge is 24 feet, with a light railing; its surface is protected by a gravel cement. Such is the Cascade Bridge, whose simple symmetrical form would perhaps conceal the effect of its vastness, were it not *set* in such a stupendous chasm. Of this chasm we must say a word, for the preparation of the gulf for the erection of the bridge appears nearly as wonderful as the structure itself. We have said that the walls of the ravine are of solid rock. The west side rises almost a sheer precipice, while the east, immediately under the bridge, is more sloping. Both sides were originally covered with a dense grove of hemlock, such as you see just above the bridge. To remove this was a Herculean task, as was also the excavation of the rock for the support of the arch. Here, then, we see the bare, steep rock of the west side completely shorn of vegetation, with nothing but tree-stumps, standing out like  bosses from its breast-plate of stone. On the west side a vast pile of broken rock slopes down to the stream, choked up with stony rubbish, and huge trees hurled there from the heights above. Some old tressels still protrude from this *debris*, and the whole appearance of the "wreck of matter" attests the violent birth whence sprung the fair and secure fabric overhead. The best general view of the bridge and chasm is the one we present from the

quarry below, on the west side, whence most of the stone for the Starrucca Viaduct was procured. The view of the bridge from the bed of the creek is obscured by the thick foliage, but still the glimpses it affords, though but partial, are very striking.

But you will ask, Why *Cascade* Bridge? In rainy weather you will ask, *Where is* the cascade? for the diminished volume of the fall that confers its title to the bridge can not make itself heard, loud as it is, through the dense thicket of hemlock that muffles its "quiet tune," save when the skies give it a full, whole choral band. The cascade is a few yards above the bridge, but entirely concealed, unless you scramble down a succession of rocky ledges, and get a close look at one of the most beautiful water-falls imaginable, about 30 feet high when the current is full, but merely streaking with white rills the green rocks when the clouds refuse the proper supplies. Another cascade, of thread-like proportions, takes the ravine at one single leap from a point between the great fall and the bridge; but they are both invisible, except to tourists willing to risk their necks for a glimpse at their coy beauties. It is to be hoped the wood concealing them may soon be thinned out, and the picturesque attractions of the spot be allowed a fair chance with the grand and wonderful. A light, secure stairway, leading down the ledges of rock near the great cascade, would be also a valuable improvement. At present there are obstacles to a general thronging of visitors, owing to the untamed wildness of the chasm and the want of suitable accommodations in the neighborhood. Were the improvements suggested carried out, and a neat, comfortable public house established in the grove below the bridge, the Cascade Bridge would be a favorite resort to tourists and pleasure parties during summer.

Some persons think the Cascade Ravine might have been crossed in a less expensive and more enduring way by *filling it in*. A glance at the chasm should surely convince them of their mistake Imagine the lump of mother earth necessary to fill up that deep wrinkle in her fair cheek! Reflect on the requisite width of such a mound, and what a *culvert* —nay, a *bridge*— would need to perforate it as a vent to the stream when swollen to a torrent of resistless volume! Instead, then, of a clumsy embankment, with a culvert, perhaps, unsuited to the wants of the creek, here we have a strong and enduring bridge—a monument of skill—an arch of triumph—a wonder of the world—not marring, but heightening by contrast the romantic beauties of the ravine. Well did General Scott exclaim, after watching a heavy train cross its untrembling fabric, "The man who could throw a *cow-path* over that gulf deserves a crown!"

This bridge cost about $70,000, was a year and a half in building, and is the work of John Fowler. From the bridge, looking north, we catch the first glimpse of the Valley of the Susquehanna, which, a few yards further, bursts upon our view in all its unconcealed loveliness. Emerging from the close, tedious lane that has so long hemmed us in, we run along a straight terrace cut in the mountain side 200 feet above the valley, and look down upon a landscape, the shortest glance at which will forever haunt the traveler with its vision of beauty. It seems as if this lovely river and vale had gathered their choicest charms into one gracious greeting, to cheer us after the passage of the wild and desolate mountain behind. We have attempted to convey an idea of the sweet features of this remarkable landscape, but what pencil or pen can portray the soul and essence of the beauty wrapped in their delicious hues—the pastoral repose brooding over those undulating hills and fair meadows, receding in the far, misty distance, when seen under an autumnal sky? The swelling mass of the wooded mountain on the left, with its shadowy form reflected in that broad curve of the river, contrasts well with the expanse of fields and pastures gently swelling upward on the right; and while the stream, momentarily vanishing, again lights up the distant vale with two bright links of its current, the plain immediately below us shows a snug farm-house, with its barns, orchard, and garden, and bright, green meadows dotted with cattle, that gladden the heart with a sense of the perfect peace and prosperity assuredly dwelling there. There is no wildness, no sublimity in this landscape; but there it lies, beneath that wall of hemlock over which we look, in all its quiet, gentle loveliness, sinking with an inexpressible charm into the heart of the traveler. The American landscape should be always seen in the autumn, to judge of the true extent of its magnificence; and nowhere does that glorious season light up the landscape more brilliantly than here "on Susquehanna side." Thus, fellow-traveler, we come to the scene where the graceful belt of light trees and natural shrubbery skirting each edge of the stream below, and occasionally throwing out fantastic semicircular clumps of willows into the smooth meadows, divide with their brilliant colors the warm green of the pastures from the cool blue current winding among them—where (it being a grazing region) these exquisite hues are not marred by stubble-fields, but retain their *unearthy*, delicate verdure through all seasons—where the hemlock groves scattered along the landscape relieve the

woods of their otherwise excessive brilliancy—where the amber light of autumn suffuses the whole valley, to whose "winding" river you may apply those happy lines of Rogers:

      " Like a silver zone
    Thrown about carelessly, it shines afar,
    Catching the eye in many a broken link,
    In many a turn and traverse as it glides.'

Fortunately, the length of the high embanked terrace whence we see this famous landscape, and the check put upon our steed by the considerate engineer, allow us full time to observe all its beauties, over which we would fain linger. The inexorable hemlock, however, at last shuts out the vision, and we lose sight of the river altogether while cutting through the base of the mountain we have been skirting. Dreary, deep sand-banks and shattered timber are all we see in this winding cut; but its termination brings us before another superb prospect, of a character different from the enchanting scene just left. Here we have the first view of the

STARRUCCA VIADUCT (from New York 190 miles, from Dunkirk 270 miles), which, even at this distance (one mile), when sunset lights up its arches, sheds a peculiar

dignity and splendor over the landscape. The valley immediately below us shows its recent redemption by its black stumps and uncultivated knolls; but beyond these are meadows and groves betokening an old settlement, together with the outline of a village placed at the base of the noble hills that inclose this grand prospect on every side. A run of two miles from the Cascade Bridge brings us to the viaduct, that takes its name from the Starrucca Creek, that here, issuing from a vale of the same title, runs into the Susquehanna. This magnificent structure is the greatest work of art along the rail-road, and ranks among the first works of its kind in this country. It is 1200 feet long, 110 feet high, and has 18 arches with

spans of 50 feet. Its body is 24 feet in width, but the top is 30 feet, affording space enough for a double track. Its appearance would be much improved by a parapet; but this deficiency is somewhat remedied by an iron railing on each side. Like the Cascade Bridge, the viaduct can not be seen to advantage unless you descend, and view it from various points below. The best of these is at the northeast angle, whence the beautifully-curved arches, and light, though substantial piers, recede from the eye in exquisite symmetry. On the west side numerous shanties and other common-place buildings obstruct the view very much; but from the opposite side of the Susquehanna an unobstructed view can be had of its whole length, as, like a huge centipede, it puts down its many feet across the

Starrucca Vale. The creek passes under one arch near its southern end, and is famous for the excellent trout in its waters higher up. Below the bridge it serves several mills, supporting the small community here, and crosses the valley to the river completely hidden in a dense grove of elm, birch, and willows. The stone of which the viaduct is built was brought partly from above on the creek, and partly from the quarry we saw at the Cascade Bridge, and has proved a good material. The whole work was intrusted to Mr. Kirkwood, the late efficient superintendent of the road, who executed his great trust within a twelve month from its commencement. The entire cost of the structure was $320,000. The viaduct, like the

Cascade Bridge, was deemed unnecessary by the advocates of the *filling-in* process; but, though very expensive, it is undoubtedly the cheapest and most durable mode of carrying the road over this ravine; and who can regret the choice that adds such a noble architectural feature to the attractions of nature and art in this particular region, where haply cluster the great monuments of the enterprise and liberality of the company.

The view from the viaduct is very imposing, for the mountains rise around us like a circle of giants, and the valley has recovered the smile of cultivation with which it first welcomed us. Looking south, we see above the richest of groves the village of Lanesborough, with its *tressle bridge*, over which we pass in a few minutes, our elevation enabling us to look down the chimneys of that community. This *tressle bridge* is 450 feet long, and 70 feet above the Canewacta Creek, that here issues from a narrow glen, and is also a tributary to the Susquehanna.

In any other part of the road this beautiful fabric would excite a sensation; but near the two structures just passed, its interest lies chiefly in the effect of carrying us over the "white, upturned gaze of wondering" villagers, that rush to their doors and watch our lofty transit above their heads. At this point the Susquehanna, so long hidden, suddenly sweeps into view through meadows extending beyond the village, and touches close on our right, to remain our companion for many miles. Just before reaching the Starrucca Viaduct we again entered the Quaker state, into which commonwealth the Susquehana here drops a graceful loop, called the *Great Bend*. *Lanesborough*, therefore, is a village of Susquehanna county, in that state. It contains some 300 or 400 inhabitants, has several mills and tanneries, and two hotels.

From Lanesborough we enter a long, straight rocky cut of a mile, quite close to the Susquehanna, that flows rapidly and clearly 30 feet below us, though we have nearly finished the descent of the grade of 60 feet from Summit. Huge buttresses of gray rock divide us from the river, like those on the Shohola cut. Looking behind us now, we enjoy, by means of the new turn in our track, a magnificent *review* of the natural and artificial glories just passed, affording us altogether the *grandest* prospect to be met with between the Hudson and the Lake. The river, the village, the bridge, and the viaduct stretch in an unob

structed line behind us; but, to have this view in perfection, the tourist must ascend the old road, extending, over the hill above us, from the village of Lanesborough to the station of Susquehanna. The difference between these two views may be judged from our illustrations, and the vast extent given to the prospect by ascending to the higher point of view was alone wanting to make it what it is, one of unsurpassed magnificence. It may be said to form an *epitome* of the glories, natural and artificial, of the New York and Erie Rail-road. From the foreground in the picture, beneath us recede the river and the rail-road, both to vanish in the dense forest of hemlock, whose varied pointed summits give such a peculiar grandeur to the distant horizon. The river, on the left, leaves us in two broad curves, one of which is rippled over by a dam, and the nearer one crossed by an old bridge, from which that yellow thread of the turnpike winds up and down the slopes of its left bank. On the right the road starts from the bridge *over the town*, whose neat church, and old red mills, and white houses peep out from willow groves and those old gray-stemmed sycamores, and makes a beautiful and unbroken curve of three miles, to vanish in the hemlocks, where the river disappears. The unobstructed view of this section of the road is very interesting; and midway upon its thread-like track stands the great viaduct, through whose arches the sunlight falls aslant, and over whose stately form the mountains, as though determined to do justice to such a proud neighbor, gather their crests up into bold, precipitous peaks, quite unlike their adjacent *round-head* brethren. Between these two arcs of the road and river stretch the most beautiful meadows, crossed and dotted with every variety of clumps, groves, and dense avenues of trees, while the white walls of the village and scattered dwellings give an animated character to the scene, making its *composition* complete. This superb landscape should also be seen in autumn, when, though those bold hemlock hills in the distance and above the viaduct still retain their sober suit of dark green, the gentler summits are richly bronzed by the early frosts, and the motley grove skirting the Starrucca Creek spans the golden green expanse of meadow like a rainbow.

Nearly two miles from Lanesborough we arrive at the Susquehanna station (from New York 192½ miles, from Dunkirk 267½ miles), placed on a narrow strip of land between the river and the hills, that now close up on either hand. Strictly the name of this locality is Harmony; but what was once a mere collection of huts, with a little public house, is now an important *depôt* or *hospital* for disabled engines and cars, and stables for those in daily use. The necessary buildings for such an establishment, where engines and cars are repaired, of course make this an important and bustling place, in addition to the less noisy business of a *station*. The engine house here is a substantial tenement, and in its neat *stables* has accom-

modations for 16 of these *metal* steeds. The number of hands employed is about 60; and their wants, and those of the engine drivers and firemen who end their day's work here, have caused the erection of spacious boarding-houses and a few tasty cottages along the hill overhanging the *depôt*. The locality has been laid off into lots, and no doubt a thriving village will soon spring up round this new head-quarters of Vulcan. A new hotel is to be erected, also, which will render it unnecessary for travelers to be jolted two miles over a rough road, in a rude car, before gaining Lanesborough.

We are now at the bottom of the descent from Summit,

and enter upon the lightest grade of the road, extending as far as Hornellsville. The ascent on this section, going west, is nowhere over *five* feet to the mile. We also, at this point, bid adieu to the grand and romantic scenery of the road, though we shall find before us much that is picturesque. This is the character of the Susquehanna where we cross its rapid current, half a mile beyond the station, by a wooden covered bridge 800 feet long, with one span of 186, and four others of 150 feet. There are actually *two* bridges, joined by a wooded island in the stream, whose

wild trees and the high hills around make the spot very picturesque. The country around this point has been famous as a hunting field, and many are the stories told by the old Nimrod that "keeps" the bridge of not only hunting deer and game, but also of the sterner sport of hunting bears and panthers, that not long since abounded in the adjacent forest. It is said deer are often seen swimming the Susquehanna near the bridge.

Our course now lies on the right bank of the river, that leads us a winding course among the hills, though now and then we bolt from its company. We are very little above its surface, and the work for five miles is very light. At that point, however, we pass through several rock-cuttings, where the views are truly beautiful. The last of

these "cuts" shows a steep face of rock about 74 feet in height, the last resistance of the soil we encounter for very many miles. Leaving the river here, we rush across a fertile plain, again to touch its banks at a point affording one of its choicest landscapes, whence, looking southwest, we have one of the finest views the Susquehanna affords.

In its distance rises a high conical mountain, at the base of which lies the village of Great Bend, in Pennsylvania. In a few minutes we stop at the station bearing the same name.

GREAT BEND (from New York $200\frac{1}{2}$ miles, from Dun-

kirk 259½ miles), eight miles from Susquehanna, and one mile to the north of its pretty namesake on the opposite side of the river. A large covered bridge crosses the Susquehanna, beyond which the village is seen, well situated,

and making quite a show with its large hotel and spacious stores. The station is one of the most important along the road, for it is placed at a great converging point of trade with the thriving towns in Pennsylvania, such as Montrose, Tunkhannock, &c.

The "Ligget's Gap" Rail-road, nearly completed, runs from this point into the Lackawanna coal region, from which it is expected to supply all Western and Central New York with anthracite via the Erie road. In the same vicinity are the great iron works of the Messrs. Scranton, who are making forty tons of rail-road iron per day. The freight-houses show the amount of business transacted here, and the numerous new stores springing up near it proves its destiny as a future rival to the opposite village. Leaving Great Bend, we run northward through a country whose fields and numerous cross-roads show that we are entering a more cultivated region. At the end of four miles we leave Pennsylvania for the last time, and enter the empire state midway in Broome county, which we first approached at Deposit. This county was first settled in 1790, chiefly by persons from Massachusetts, though a French colony had settled on the Chenango in 1787. It was little known before the Revolution, and until within a few years held a population of *lumbermen*. Since the introduction of roads and canals, it has advanced in agricultural importance, and in the richness and abundance of its products now vies with Orange. Though generally mountainous, there is hardly a hill not susceptible of cultivation to the very top. The same, however, may be said of the entire Valley of the Susquehanna in this region. Its sudden growth is prodigious, for in the numerous large towns we shall soon approach, many of the settlers are still living that first visited them in canoes. As we advance along this fine valley, the evidences of a fertile soil and greater population become evident, though the scenery proportionally becomes monotonous, and the road, running through a level plain, presents nothing of interest in its construction.

KIRKWOOD (from New York 206 miles, from Dunkirk 254 miles) is a small village, so called after a former superintendent of the road. In this neighborhood, on the north side of the road, stands an old, shabby wooden house, that may be some day looked upon with great reverence, propped up with tenderest care, and visited by troops of pilgrims to view its hallowed timbers. It is the house in which was born *Joe Smith*, the Mormon prophet. Yes, that shabby tenement was Joe's cradle, and may be some day the thronged *Mecca* to his disciples from the mighty West. The signs of increasing cultivation and prosperity in the farms we pass are gradually mingled with the unmistakable evidences of a large town being near. We see successively wagon-loads of town goods, then elegant town vehicles containing town-dressed people, and then elegant suburban residences, proofs of the wealth and taste of the community we approach, and that is

BINGHAMTON (from New York 216 miles, from Dunkirk 245 miles). This beautiful village, the largest and fairest community on the main line of the road we have met

since leaving New York city, is situated in a wide plain, and on an angle formed by the confluence of the Susquehanna and the Chenango Rivers. It was named after its original settler, Mr. Bingham, an Englishman, who died in 1804, leaving two daughters, afterward married to Alexander Baring and his brother Henry, the famous English bankers of that name, one of whom, it is well known, was afterward created Lord Ashburton. Binghamton at once sprang into importance by its being so happily placed on two such streams, whose lumber and water-power forthwith formed the elements of its prosperity. Besides these mills, the Chenango Canal, extending along that river 95 miles to Utica, proved the next auspicious source of improvement for Binghamton. The flour trade by this canal is extensive. That work, however, has somewhat languished under the superior advantages afforded by the Erie Rail-road, that has given the crowning impulse to the business of Binghamton, and thus we find it a busy town, containing some 5000 inhabitants. The station is built on an open area north of the town, and its offices, freight-houses, and perfect maze of "turn-outs," "switches," &c., covered with trains and freight-cars, prove it one of first importance. The village covers several hundred acres, and boasts many fine streets planted with trees, and ornamented with some half dozen churches, the county buildings, and several excellent hotels. The side-walks are made of plank, and prove both neat and convenient. The canal passing through the town gives, with its boats and bridges, a peculiar character to the streets. A long wooden bridge connects the main business part with the suburbs on the south side of the Susquehanna, as several others do with the west side of the Chenango, where the elegant private residences of the older and more opulent citizens are seen, with beautiful gardens and trees sloping down to the water's side. Standing on one of these bridges over the Chenango at sunset, and looking either north or south along these garden shores, the traveler will be struck with the beauty of the scene. Washington Irving has pronounced them unsurpassed in any village he has ever visited. On the southern side of the Susquehanna, and directly opposite the junction of the Chenango, there is also, from the garden of Mr. Eldridge, an interesting view of the town; and a ride down the main street, on the west bank of the Chenango, will also show the elegant taste of the citizens in architecture and ornamental grounds. The best general view of Binghamton and the valley is to be had from a hill south of the town, which we have selected as showing the course of the two rivers and the *massing* of the town most effectively. The drives in this direction afford an endless variety of extensive views of the valley. Directly west of, and near the station, the road crosses the Chenango by a wooden bridge of great length and of va-

ried design. Either end of it is covered. Under the eastern portion the Chenango Canal passes.

Chenango, in Indian, is said by some to mean "Beautiful" or "Pleasant Waters," while others contend that it means "Swift River." Whichever be the true signification, the word will be well applied, for a swifter or more beautiful river never ran toward the sea.

With such a position, in such a fertile plain, and with such rapid means of connection with New York and all the minor points of trade surrounding it, what can prevent Binghamton from growing into an inland metropolis? Looking back at its comparatively recent settlement, what a still greater change may be anticipated. Before the numerous roads were opened for its only business, *lumber*, its only market was Philadelphia. In 1810 there was but one mail per week from New York. With this anticipated growth of Binghamton, it has a community whose intelligence, enterprise, and refined taste will keep pace with its increasing wealth. There is no place where hospitality and social intercourse are conducted in a more liberal and refined manner. It will never be forgotten with what spirit its citizens got up the celebration of the opening of the road to this place, on the 27th of December, 1848, which, though the elements rather combined to make a late collation, yet proved at the same time the warmth of a reception which no frosts could chill or paralyze.

A good academy, two or three female seminaries, and liberal public school advantages offer additional inducements for settling in Binghamton. Plank roads are being extended in every direction, which will undoubtedly secure a large amount of trade that has heretofore gone to Utica and Syracuse. A large business must naturally come from Pennsylvania, and hence it needs no prophet's eye to discover a rapid and healthy growth for the town.

This place has some excellent hotels, the chief of which, the Lewis House, near the station, will be found equal to the best in the land in point of accommodations. Some distance up the Chenango a colony of French settled in 1790. Talleyrand visited it in 1795, and took his private secretary from that place. The colony was afterward broken up and scattered.

Upon the site of Binghamton, a brigade of American troops, in 1779, under the command of General James Clinton, the father of De Witt Clinton, encamped for one or two nights, on their way to join the main body under Sullivan, then penetrating westward. The first white man who made a permanent settlement in what is claimed for the village vicinity was Captain Joseph Leonard, who was from Plymouth, Massachusetts. Soon after came Colonel William Rose, from Connecticut, and then Whitneys, from Columbia county. At the time of their settlement (1787) their nearest white neighbors were at Tioga, a distance of 40 miles.—Vide *Wilkinson's Annals of Binghamton*, 1840.

In the same annals is mentioned how, in consequence of a freshet in 1794, a great scarcity was felt, during which a Major Stow shouldered a bushel of wheat, in which the whole neighborhood had a common share, and started for Wattle's Ferry to mill, a distance of more than 40 miles, carrying his grist the whole distance on foot. On his return the neighbors held a sort of thanksgiving over their "*short-cake*" and a pound of tea he had purchased, and, as they had no *hog's lard*, they substituted *bear's grease* to make their cake tender.

Beyond Binghamton the country continues of the same level, rich character, with but few glimpses of the river to relieve its monotony. The observant traveler will, on this section of the road, remark for the first time a double row of half-decayed posts along the left of the road, now buried in the soil, now rising above it ten feet, now hugging our track, now bolting off at a tangent across the valley, now dark and decayed, and now fresh and strong enough to bear bridges (evidently never used) twenty feet long! This is a puzzling apparition to the stranger; and if you read the early history of this rail-road, you will understand how, to the eyes of a stockholder, each of these black posts is a dismal monument to the memory of millions sunk in sinking their never-used timbers, and how those bridges are indeed veritable "bridges of sighs." When the New York and Erie Rail-road, under the stimulus of the state loan, was begun at the Dunkirk terminus, and was in progress throughout almost its entire length in 1841, 90 miles of it, between Binghamton and Hornellsville, were "piled" with these upright posts, on which the road was to rest, to be *filled in* underneath. To effect this, an ingenious machine was invented and put in operation, to *drive* and *saw off* these *piles* with dispatch; and it is melancholy to turn to the "journals of the day," and see the enthusiastic records of the daily progress of this wonderful driver and cutter, as though every post driven was an additional support on which was to rest the future fortunes of the villages along the route! Ninety miles were thus *posted up*, when the treasury of the company became embarrassed, the work was stopped, and the road at the point of death, when it was resuscitated by calling in new nurses and physicians. When the work was again started, new and improved modes of engineering showed that it would be actually cheaper to throw aside the *piled* route as useless, and run a new line. This was done, and the track was laid as it now is, leaving the said outposts to remain unused, a homely imitation of a Roman viaduct, stretching mournfully across a wide campagna!

Keeping along the Susquehanna Valley, that remains the same in rich cultivation as we pass westward, our next stopping-place is

UNION (from New York 223 miles, from Dunkirk 237 miles), *nine* miles beyond Binghamton. The station stands half a mile from the village that names it, a good view of which. and the singular round hill adjacent, may be had

from the station. Union is a thriving little village of about 1000 inhabitants, standing in the midst of a broad plain as Binghamton does, though half a mile distant from the Susquehanna. The high round hill spoken of slopes up from the main street, and affords a fine pasture to its very top, excepting on its southern face, which is very precipitous, and covered with pine and hemlock. From its summit there are superb views up and down the valley for many miles, showing the windings of the river, while immediately below us its current is broken up with small islands, fringed with trees, and molded in every variety of fantastic shape. These islands are rich pasturages, and have on them herds of cattle and flocks of geese, that add much to the quiet rural beauty of the river. Union was settled in 1789 by one Judge Mersereau, of Tioga county. He served with distinction under Washington, who intrusted to his keeping certain British officers after Burgoyne's surrender. The judge's wife entered so fully into his attempt to make the captives comfortable, that she finally eloped with the youngest of the unfortunate prisoners. In spite of this unfortunate act of *disunion* on the part of his wife, the judge conferred upon his new settlement its present patriotic title.

The flats around Union are very fertile, and one mile in width. These extend several miles before us, and through them the Nanticoke Creek passes toward Susquehanna. We cross its small stream by a wooden bridge. There are several mills on this creek in sight. At this point we touch the base of the mountains closely, while the "flats" still keep on our left. The turnpike from Bing-

hamton to Owego passes along the mountain also, and from many of its high points overlooks the road and the river. From one of these points, three miles beyond Union, the view is really superb as we look westward, and see the round hill near that village rising, mound-like, from the vast plain, while immediately below us the Susquehanna, by one of its graceful curves, sweeps closely up alongside of the rail-road, winding thread-like round the heights on the left. Leaving this exquisite bit of scenery, we soon enter a region directly opposite in character, and of almost primitive nature, the only marks of man's presence being such as to make the prospect more desolate, for those cleared patches on the hill side, with their gloomy hemlock and black stumps, in showery weather make the prospect appear as though it had been desolated by war Presently we catch sight of a long new bridge over the

Susquehanna, and the busy-looking factories of Apalachin on the opposite side of the river.

Here we leave Broome county and enter Tioga, once a part of that now called Chemung. The eastern portion of its soil resembles that of Broome, but the northwestern abounds in limestone and gypsum.

CAMPVILLE (from New York 230 miles, from Dunkirk 230 miles) is six and a half miles from Union, and will become, ere long, of importance, from the quantity of cattle brought here to be sent to New York. The village is an old-fashioned one, but boasting a hotel which it would be well for larger places to imitate in point of cleanliness,

comfortable beds, and good fare. This station is just equidistant from New York and Dunkirk.

From Campville a remarkable embanked curve in the road follows the river side, and then, rushing across a wide plain by a straight section, in length only second to

that at Delaware, we suddenly come upon the pretty village of

OWEGO (from New York 236½ miles, from Dunkirk 223½ miles). The station and offices here, like the town itself, are next in rank to Binghamton, to which Owego bears much resemblance, though not possessing the natural advantages of position which Binghamton enjoys. It is

named after the creek on which it stands, at its junction with the Susquehanna, though Mr. Willis asserts the name should be written Ow*a*go—that is, "swift river," the very translation given by some to the word *Chenango*. But, indeed, there is much uncertainty and fancy in these same translations, for we have often heard half a dozen meanings assigned to some of the aboriginal terms. Like Binghamton, Owego is placed in a level, fertile part of the valley, and on the margin of the Susquehanna, here crossed by a wooden bridge. The first clearing was made in 1791,

and the village was incorporated in 1827. Its growth was very rapid, its wealth mainly springing from the salt-springs of Salina, which staple, with lumber, were sent down to Pennsylvania and Maryland. Mills, too, flourished on the Owego, and finally the rail-road fully opened to it an enriching channel of business. It now contains about 2500 inhabitants, and possesses all the appurtenances of an important town in its banks, printing-offices, churches, and busy hotels. There are also several flour, plaster, and woolen mills here. The business done is large, and its streets and stores appear always crowded. The new part of the town is planted with trees, and lined with plank pavements, and ornamented with beautiful dwellings, as Binghamton is. This pretty village received a severe loss by the great fire in the autumn of 1849, when nearly all its large stores, its bank, several hotels (and a part of the bridge over the Susquehanna), forming one third of the town, were consumed. The loss of property, though great, did not prove fatal, for immediately the energy and enterprise of the citizens caused new edifices to appear on the ashes of the burned district. The rapid growth of Owego is seen in the fact that, at the opening of the road in 1849, the man was present that put up the first log hut on the spot where the town now stands ! From Owego the Cayuga and Susquehanna Rail-road extends to Ithaca, on Cayuga Lake, a distance of 30 miles, having a gauge of the same width with the parent road; and by this branch road an important addition has been made to the business of the main road and to Owego, by the trade opened with the northern counties by the lake, that send down their plaster, flour, and other produce for the lumber, coal, iron, and other staples of the southern. The travel, too, is large, as it furnishes a speedier and more varied route to those who have heretofore traveled by the way of Albany to New York.

The country around Owego is exceedingly beautiful, and affords fine drives. Several of the proprietors of the surrounding land are paying great attention to improving it, so that in a short time it will be one vast plain of the highest cultivation. The locality of most interest in the neighborhood of the village is Glen Mary, the late rural abode of N. P. Willis, whose graceful pen has bestowed on its beauties an immortality that will always make the spot attractive to tourists. The house has "gone to strangers," but the attractions of the retreat remain precisely as when the late owner penned the "Letters from under a Bridge"—where, by-the-way, his humble seat now lies unused, and dusty by the showers of "free soil" through the crevices of the bridge. The *glen*, so called, is more like a gentle ravine than the species of vale which that Highland title designates. A little brook leaps down through its thick groves, and near one of its prettiest cascades is the grave of Mr. Willis's infant child—a fit and touching resting-place for it, beside that young and hurrying streamlet. From a hill just above the house there is a superb view, in the middle-ground of which, between two sloping outlines of mountains, Owego is very picturesquely placed.

The road passes Owego Creek by a substantial bridge, half a mile west of Owego, and then resumes the course along the valley, varying but little from its general character.

SMITHBOROUGH (from New York 246 miles, from Dunkirk 214 miles) is a prettily-situated village, on the right side of the road, 10 miles beyond Owego. A bridge cross-

es the Susquehanna here on the left. As we proceed onward, the country evidently becomes less settled and quite uninteresting.

BARTON (from New York 249 miles, from Dunkirk 211 miles) is a thriving little town, beautifully situated, three miles beyond Smithborough. It has a respectable business, although the station is yet in its infancy, and has several good hotels. The old road ran through this town to the north of the present one, and from  one of its substantial unused bridges we take the accompanying sketch.

A few miles beyond Barton we take one last look at the Susquehanna, which, however, before leaving, bestows a bit of its scenery upon us almost as wild as that on the Delaware. It has brought us quite to the edge of Pennsylvania again, but, declining to follow the sharp elbow it thrusts across the "line," we cross the base of its angle, and keep due on through one of the

straightest sections and most level plains on the road. A little further we cross a high embankment thrown across the flat vale through which the Cayuta Creek flows. Two

bridges afford a passage to its waters, that have caused to spring up there, to the north of us, the busy mills that give to the village the name of Factoryville.

WAVERLEY (from New York 266 miles, from Dunkirk 194 miles), as the station at this place is called, is situated in a deep curved cut, half a mile from the end of the

embankment, and one mile from the old village, that has attained great business activity, and is as thriving as any community we have passed.

The neat little village of Waverley stands on a hill to the west of Factoryville, though what has caused it to spring up there no one can imagine. The *station* is destined to be an important one. Already, since it was sketched for this work, has it changed its appearance to a degree perfectly marvelous, so that what was a twelve-month since a simple station-house almost hidden by the banks of the rail-road, is now the nucleus of a bustling mass of stores and public houses.

Very near the station the traveler will be struck with a bare, flat-topped, regularly-shaped mound, 110 feet above

the surrounding soil, which is here called Spanish Hill—*why* is an unsolved riddle. Its shaven, regular slope, and certain marks on the top, show that at one time it had been fortified—possibly during the old French war, and thus its foreign birth might have got confounded. It is, however, the subject of a legend—an article lamentably scarce in these regions, that want the charm of *association* to keep one unfatigued while traversing its eternal sameness. According to the legend, on one occasion a party of six Indians encamped on this hill, with three white prisoners carried off from the massacre of Wyoming. At night the captives rose and slew five of their captors, the sixth escaping. Upon this simple brave achievement has been embroidered a tissue of bloody, supernatural, and ridiculous stories. It is said that, in consequence of the triumph of the captive whites, the Indians believed no red man could leave that hill alive. The pale faces, also, have their awful suspicions about the mount, as some swear that the devil himself has been seen running up and down it; and others, again, believe that Captain Kidd's treasure—those very ubiquitous depostes!—was buried in its mysterious bosom.

The extremity of the tongue of land formed by the Susquehanna dipping down into Pennsylvania is called *Tioga Point*, and the *west* side of it is formed by the *Chemung* River, that here joins the former, and which last, thus enlarged, keeps on to the south. Tioga Point is a place of great natural beauty and of historical interest; for here not only did the expedition stop that afterward desolated Wyoming, but in 1779 it was the rendezvous for the forces of Generals Sullivan and Clinton, then in pursuit of *Brant*, just reeking with the blood shed at Minnisink. The village of Athens—the eternal, omnipresent Athens, to be found from St. John's to the Rio Grande!—stands on this point. The Indian name of Tioga was *Ta-hi-o-ga*, said to mean "conjunction of streams," the same translation given to many other names. It seems strange there should be such a radical difference in the dialects of tribes living so near each other! In addition to its natural and historical interest, Tioga Point is the outlet of the coal and iron mines of Pennsylvania, that are here exchanged for the lumber, plaster, and salt of New York. At the station of

CHEMUNG (from New York 260 miles, from Dunkirk 200 miles), five miles west of Waverley, we see the River *Chemung* for the first time, and find it a worthy tributary to the Susquehanna. The road runs close along the stream at this place, and at considerable height above it. Its embanked curve makes a noble section for the practical man to look at, and, looking back from the end of the embankment, the tourist may catch a view worthy of the "winding river" itself. The abundance of hemlock and the uncultivated appearance of this region show that

lumber and leather are its support. The rafts we saw constantly increasing on the Susquehanna are seen more frequently on the Chemung, and the narrow alleys in the mountain sides for sliding down the timber, so remarkable on the Delaware, are again a frequent feature of the landscape. Five miles beyond Waverley we pass through a level plain crossed by the Chemung. We pass the river by a substantial wooden bridge. Heavy gravel cuts and another level plain succeed; and then, suddenly turning westward close to the brink of the river, we pass the great rock-cutting at the *Narrows*, near Wellsburg.

The scenery is now improving, with evident signs of our getting into a region more populous.

The left bank of the river at the "Narrows" is formed by a steep mountain, along which the "cut" is made in the rock for half a mile, though the right bank is a wide,

flat meadow of great fertility, ending in the mountains half a mile from the river. A wooded island in the Chemung at this point gives more interest to the view of the Narrows. At the further end of the rocky "cut," in a little recess of the hills, stands the old village of Wellsburg.

WELLSBURG station (from New York 266 miles, from Dunkirk 194 miles) is of but little importance. Our road now enters a region, however, bearing every token of rich land and high cultivation, and after a run of seven miles through its extensive farms, we arrive at

ELMIRA (from New York 273 miles, from Dunkirk 187 miles). This is the queen city along the New York and Erie Rail-road, and is a good specimen of the towns that seem to *exhale* from the American soil. Rapid as has been the growth of Binghamton and Owego, theirs have been as a snail's pace compared with that of their Western rival. Situated on the north bank

of the Chemung, we enter its streets by a covered bridge of wood. Adjoining is the bridge over which the turnpike to Owego crosses. The traveler, as he skirts along its suburbs to its busy station in the west end, and then passes to his hotel through those compact streets, crowded with business and intersected by a canal, can hardly believe that Elmira, 20 years ago, was a little obscure village, though its settlement goes much further back. It was settled in 1788 by a Captain John Hendry. At that time it was on the only pathway from Wilkesbarre to Canada. Its original name was *Con-e-wa-wah*, or, "*head on a pole*," from the fact that the head of an Indian chief was found here thus mounted—a good, sonorous title, and far better than the present lackadaisical name of the town. Captain Hendry, however, Anglicized it into Newton. In 1791 the village was located by one Moses De Witt, and, of course, its name was again changed

—this time to *Dewittsburgh*. Under that title it figures in the original plot and conveyance. In that year the first frame house was erected. The lands were sold to settlers at eighteen pence per acre. The town finally received its present title from some gentleman who named it after his wife. Though at once made a prosperous settlement by its advantages as a lumber depôt, and the mill-seats on Newton Creek, that not far off empties into the Chemung, it did not assume remarkable growth until the construction of the Chemung Canal in 1830–32. This important work, extending 20 miles to Seneca Lake, at once supplied an outlet for its lumber by way of the Erie Canal, and brought here, in return, valuable exchanges of merchandise, to be sent in large quantities into Pennsylvania by the Williamsport and Elmira Rail-road, already in good part constructed, opening into the heart of Northern Pennsylvania. This period may be considered the beginning of its fortunes, that have flourished since to such a degree as to make it now a town containing about 5000 inhabitants, with factories, churches, academies, printing-offices, store-houses, and every other sign of a future city. It is situated in a broad valley, rivaling in fertility and beauty that in which Binghamton stands. From the high mountains half a mile west of Elmira, where the river makes a sudden bend, the best view may be had of the town and of the valley. From the dark fringe of mountains in the distance, the Chemung winds thread-like toward us, across the fertile flats, till in the center of the picture, where it flings out its broad, bright sheet, with its wooded island and bridges, on the right side of which extends afar the white and steepled mass of the town, and on the left the rich fields and groves, streaked by the yellow line of the rail-road. Nursed in the lap of such a fertile vale, every *hill* of which, even, is cultivatable to the top, and fed on the tributes of that river and that canal, no wonder Elmira at once proved a stout and

healthy young giant. These elements of prosperity received their crowning impulse by the extension of the Erie Rail-road to Elmira in October, 1849, that has opened to this magnificent and fertile valley such a direct and rapid communication with the city of New York, and, by the Newburgh branch, with the river counties. The *station*, of course, is extensive in its buildings and the amount of its business. In addition to the agent's office and freight-houses, a large engine-house, with turn-table, renders the station one of importance. Another element of prosperity to this fortunately-situated town is the branch rail-road extending from a point four miles north of Elmira to Jefferson, on Seneca Lake. In connection with the "Benjamin Loder," a fast steamer on the lake, this new route, opened in January, 1850, has not only increased the trade with the northern counties, but is a favorite route with travelers coming from the northwest and west to New York. Seneca Lake, owing to its great depth, is never frozen, and thus the communication can be kept open in winter, while the diversified character of the scenery on the Erie Rail-road must prove a great attraction to tourists, to say nothing of the time gained by this route. This branch rail-road is soon to be extended to Canandaigua, and in the course of another year to Niagara Falls. The branch road to the lake passes through a beautiful country, and the tourist visiting Elmira should not fail to take this rapid run by rail and steam to GENEVA, at the foot of the lake, for a pleasanter sail and a fairer town he will not meet on this continent. The whole region abounds with the picturesque, that makes the hackneyed titles of its fairy nooks and localities disgusting. We have already groaned over the vile taste that has rejected the expressive and sonorous Indian titles, and adopted those of the ancient and classical world; but the region round Seneca Lake has been wofully victimized by some pedant, that has emptied Lempriere's Classical Dictionary upon its devoted acres. Thus the lake itself, which the Indians called *Ho-ne-oye*, or "Hemlock Lake," was dubbed *Seneca*, though, if its philosophic depth had to be named after a Greek sage, *Socrates* had a better right, inasmuch as he is associated with one species of hemlock in his last jorum of earthly drink! Then its shores are so dotted with Ovid, Hector Falls, Homer, &c., that we expect to meet with

"Jupiter and *Cay*sar, likewise Nebucknad*nay*sar,"

and other classicalities of the "groves of Blarney." With such pedantic titles for really pretty places, disgusting our common sense and taste, it is refreshing to meet with such short aboriginal sounds as *Pen-Yan*, or the downright rough but intelligible Saxon of "*Horse-heads*"—which *means something*, and *that* is the fact that, where the village stands, General Sullivan, while encamped here in 1780, slew his old cavalry horses, and their skulls being left to whiten the plain, the place became a Golgotha of steeds, and hence its name. The mention of "*Horseheads*" reminds us of the historical event that fortunately invests *Elmira* and the neighborhood with the sacred interest associated with one of the Revolutionary battles. We have already spoken of the retreat of the Indians under Brandt after the bloody defeat of the New York troops in 1779, near the Lackawaxen, and the pursuit of the foe by an army of 5000 men under General Sullivan, that had, under orders from Washington, collected at Tioga Point, and then followed Brandt up the Chemung. The Indians, that numbered 500 on their retreat, were joined by a force of 250 British and regulars under experienced officers, and the allies then made a stand at Elmira, just in front of the bridge. At this point Brandt commanded the Indians, while the regulars were posted behind a breast-work extending to the left as far as the high mountain westward of the town, and at the base of which Newton Creek flows into the Chemung. The plans of the allies were ingenious, but could not baffle Sullivan, who, sending up the mountains a strong brigade under General Poor to turn their left flank, at the same time made a furious assault upon their breast-work. After a short struggle the allies gave way, and retreated, with great slaughter, toward Seneca Lake. Sullivan followed ; but, from some cause or other, the victory was not made decisive by any subsequent dispersion of the Indians, who not long after collected in large marauding bands. Sullivan encamped for some time at Horse-heads, six miles from Elmira, and there slew his old chargers, as already described. The point of his encampment when at Elmira was Sullivan's Mills, on Newton Creek, half a mile west of the town.

Besides this Revolutionary incident, Elmira is associated with the history of an eminent personage, above all others acquainted with strange vicissitudes of fortune, the late Louis Philippe, ex-king of the French. We have mentioned that Talleyrand had visited the Chenango Valley in 1795, and the revolution in France had also thrown on our shores at the same time the young Duke of Orleans (then the title of Louis Philippe) and his brothers, the dukes of Nemours and De Berri. These royal outcasts came to Elmira on foot from Canandaigua, and after a short stay they descended the Chemung and Susquehanna to Harrisburg. Since that era, what a change has passed over the old wily Protean minister and the exiled prince, successively the popular king and the banished monarch ! and within that epoch this (then wild) valley has leaped into a wealth, dignity, and importance that would, as a title, confer honor on king, duke, or baron.*

We can not close these reflections upon the history and growth of Elmira without quoting an amusing incident in its earliest history, as told by the ingenious Jo Sykes, and which may be regarded as prognostic of the rapid increase

* For an interesting sketch of this journey, see the Democratic Review for May, 1840.

of the community. One summer afternoon, in 1788, while Captain John Hendry (the first settler of Elmira) and his son were at work on a log hut, a man and woman emerged from the pathway leading from Newton Creek. The man rode ahead, with a basket on each side, holding a young baby. The woman was in the rear, on horseback, surrounded with the goods and chattels of the family. The man approached, and asked if a doctor was to be had near, and to the colonel's questions replied that his wife had hurt herself by stumbling. Learning that no physician was in the neighborhood, they passed on further, and made themselves the best shelter they could get that night. Next morning the colonel again met the man near the spot, and inquired after his wife's health. "As well as could be expected," was the answer. The following day Hendry sent his son to inquire about them, and the boy returned saying that they were preparing to start. "But the poor woman, my son, how is she?" "Oh!" replied the boy, "oh! she's got *another* baby, and I guess she wants another basket to put it in!"

Beyond Elmira we cross the Chemung, and pass *Junction* with the Chemung Rail-road, four miles from Elmira (from New York $277\frac{1}{2}$ miles, from Dunkirk $182\frac{1}{2}$ miles). The length of the Chemung Rail-road is eighteen miles. From its terminus the Jefferson and Canandaigua Railroad, soon to be opened, is 45 miles in length, and arrangements are now making to extend it to Niagara Falls. The company has been organized and the surveys have been made.

BIG FLATS (from New York $283\frac{1}{2}$ miles, from Dunkirk $176\frac{1}{2}$ miles) is a small station. A village is springing up around it.

CORNING (from New York 291 miles, from Dunkirk 169 miles), 17 miles beyond Elmira. This thriving town stands on the south bank of the Chemung River, and contains about 1500 inhabitants. It is beautifully situated at the foot of a noble hill, affording fine views of the rich valley. It has several large hotels, a foundery, and fac-

tories, and is the depôt of the Corning and Blossburg Railroad, that extends 40 miles to a rich field of bituminous coal, the only one known to exist near the line of our state, wherein such coal is in extensive demand. The feeder of the Chemung Canal extends from Elmira to this place. This is perhaps the greatest lumbering depôt we have yet met in our journey along this timber region. It is reckoned that twenty-five millions of feet of dressed timber are sent down every year from this place; and thus one can imagine what a blessing a rapid transit by rail must prove to such a depôt. The Chemung is here very wide, and is crossed by a covered wooden bridge. Like Elmira and Owego, Corning has felt the ravages of fire, almost the entire business portion of the village having been burned in 1850; but, like its burned sisters, it has risen from its ashes in greater and more substantial beauty and enterprise. Whole blocks of brick houses stand now where before frail frame buildings and shanties only were seen. At this point commences the Buffalo and Conhocton Valley Rail-road, whose construction is just commenced. It is expected to be completed by August, 1851, to the pleasant village of Bath, and early in 1852 to be completed to Buffalo. It will be an important branch of our road. Its length will be about 135 miles. On the opposite side of the river are the two communities of *Knoxville* and *Centerville*. The former is composed of lumbermen, living in shanties. There is an inviting field of labor for the missionaries in these lumbering villages. Nearly two miles west of Corning the Chemung divides into two forks, the northern one of which is called the *Conhocton*, and the southern the *Canisteo*—the former (so said) signifying "trees in the water," and the latter " board in the water." One mile from Corning we cross the Chemung by a long wooden bridge of several arches. We soon perceive the junction of the two rivers. The scenery there is very beautiful, and through the large trees that overhang them we have taken the glimpse here given of the pretty village of

PAINTED POST (from New York $292\frac{1}{2}$ miles, from Dunkirk $167\frac{1}{2}$ miles). This beautiful little retired village is by far the oldest settlement in this inland part, and is said

to date its existence as far back as 200 years since. Consequently there is a sober dignity in its appearance, but at the same time its hotels, spacious stores, and neat dwellings prove that it keeps pace with the progress of the present age. It derives its name from the fact that a painted post was found here over the grave of a celebrated Indian chief, in the very part of the open area of the village where a high modern post, striped with red and white paint, now stands, surmounted with a painted metal outline of an Indian chief with raised arrow, to perpetuate the legend. The villagers regard this monument with great reverence, and are jealous of all heresy as to the true locality of this legend, scorning the pretensions of the little community (Centerville) between them and Corning, which, claiming its locality to be the true one for the aboriginal monument, has also erected for itself a painted post, and, in order to eclipse the sheet iron statue of its bigger rival, has capped *its* wooden pillar with a board having an Indian painted on each side. Now, though the Centervillians have thus taken a *double* chance upon the decision of the traveler, yet the more durable effigy, *exclusively metallic*, of Painted Post seems to look more authentic than the perishable tawny that stares at you from the painted sides of the Centerville sign-board. There is a spurious, parvenu imitative complexion in the latter post too—its delicate pink, more like a stick of mint candy, that makes one regard with confidence its rival's ensanguined hues! Indeed, the high-*metalled* hero revolving at its top—*vane*-est of weather-cocks!—seems to utter this sentiment as we view him at a distance, his pointed arrow looking as if he had his thumb to his nose, and with expanded digits he were saying to his rival, "You can't come it! I am the only true and original Painted Post—I am!"

At this interesting, time-honored point in our road we must now close our particular description and illustrations of the country through which passes the New York and Erie Rail-road. True, it is now about to be opened to its western terminus, and before these pages meet your eye, the dusky banner of its iron ships will stream upon the shores of Lake Erie. Until that great completion is effected, we will reserve our detailed notices of the portion now in operation beyond the point where we fold up notes and sketch-book. In the mean time, we will say that the road as far as Hornellsville, running as it does along the banks of the Canisteo, presents little variety in its scenery, or passes through no villages of note or importance. It is throughout a vast timber region; but agricultural resources will soon be developed to a degree to make it speedily assume the rich, smiling aspect of the valley of the Chemung. Though not varied, its scenery at times assumes the grand character of the Delaware, set off with a few graceful reminiscences of the Susquehanna. To the eye of one unfamiliar with the hemlock region, its vast groves of that somber tree clothing its precipitous mountains would prove an impressive spectacle indeed.

The detailed description of the remainder of the road, and sketches of objects and scenery most worthy the notice of the traveler, must be reserved for another edition. In the unfinished state of the work at this time (November, 1850), it is impossible for the artist to sketch such views as would be best adapted for a work of this kind, and the descriptions of the road itself, the stations, and all the belongings, would necessarily be imperfect.

At this point, then, fellow-traveler, we leave you to roll alone over the road to Dunkirk. We would fain accompany you, and show by pen and pencil the fruits our more leisurely steps had picked up along this as yet unopened route, to make your information of this interesting region less vague and hurried than your rapid progress unavoidably makes it. But, ere we part, will you not agree with us that a route lying through a more diversified or interesting region can be nowhere traversed than the track we have just run over? The strawberry-patches and mountain-forges of Rockland; the dairy-pastures of Orange; the wild Delaware, with its wilder raftsmen, its leather and its game; the gentle Susquehanna, with its pastures, and grain, and civilization; and, finally, the Chemung, with its exhaustless timber and herds of cattle—what more varied region than this in productive fertility, more sublime and beautiful in scenery, or more interesting in historic associations? Thus much in respect to the country; and does not the road itself stand forth a proud and worthy highway for so glorious a district? Its magnificent scale, its daring enterprise, its triumphant engineering skill over unprecedented obstacles, not only of nature, but of a kind almost as formidable—prejudice, and ill-willed croakers, to say nothing of opposition of a political character, justly put it above all other undertakings of a similar nature. Besides its main glory as the great connecting link between New York and Lake Erie, thereby bringing the mighty granaries and herds of Ohio and Michigan by three days' transit to the great market of the Union, this rail-road has acted with peculiar beneficence upon the varied regions it traverses. Its blessings upon the southern counties have proved two-fold. Not only has it poured a vast trade and travel along its extent, and brought ready and never-failing liberal purchasers for the produce that once lay in almost waste profusion among its inaccessible sections, but it has opened to rapid access districts previously almost unknown, or at least lying uncultivated, in all its primitive wildness, with but a scant and not very orderly population. Thus, while such old refined regions as those of Orange and around Binghamton can now find a ready market for their produce, such primeval tracts as those along the Delaware and the Chemung have for the first time their rugged solitudes invaded by this glorious harbinger of all the blessings of civilization. The wild, unsettled habits of the lumbermen must yield to the influence of the plow, which bringing Plenty, Education will close up the beneficent train. Here, then, is the happy means of intercourse between adjacent counties once unknown to each other—a small but important link in that precious chain of social intimacy so essential to the *sincerity* and stability of our Union, and for the extension of which so much has been done by the New York and Erie Rail-road.

Taking up our journey where we left it at the close of the description of the portion of the road completed at the time it was written, we will give the traveler such scanty information as we possess relative to the country he passes through to the termination of the road.

ADDISON (from New York $301\frac{1}{2}$ miles, from Dunkirk $158\frac{1}{2}$ miles) is pleasantly situated at the confluence of the Canisteo River and Tuscarora Creek. Its population is about 1500. It is the center of a large trade, principally in lumber, and is one of the busiest and most business-like places along the road. The Tuscarora Valley furnishes an avenue through which a large portion of the country can approach the rail-road at this place. A plank road up the valley is in progress, through which a large part of the county of Tioga, in Pennsylvania, will find a market here. Addison was originally named Middletown, and was organized in 1796. Its early inhabitants attended church at Canandaigua, eight miles distant. Following up the gentle stream of the Canisteo, the next station we approach, after a run of five miles, is

RATHBONEVILLE (from New York $306\frac{1}{2}$ miles, from Dunkirk $153\frac{1}{2}$ miles). It is a pretty village of about 400 inhabitants, and takes its name from the principal proprietor. A valuable agricultural district, lying south of the Canisteo, comes to the rail-road at this place.

CAMERON (from New York 314 miles, from Dunkirk 146 miles) is a very small village lying on the Canisteo, and contains between 200 and 300 inhabitants. This portion of the road is passed over so rapidly that little opportunity is given for inspection of the villages, and there are few natural objects worthy of notice. The country is rather sparsely settled, but the opening of the rail-road will soon bring population.

CANISTEO (from New York 327½ miles, from Dunkirk 132½ miles) is an unimportant station, but surrounded by a fertile country. A rapid run of four miles brings us to the termination of the level grade we have been traveling over for the last hundred and forty miles, and we reach

HORNELLSVILLE (from New York 331½ miles, from Dunkirk 128½ miles), a station of considerable importance. The village is happily situated in one of the wide areas of the valley, where the hills recede from the river, and in that respect it starts with the same natural advantages of position enjoyed by Elmira and other towns. The station is about a mile east of the village, on the finest portion of the level plain. The depôt buildings are rather imposing in their appearance. Another village is already growing up around the depôt. The company employ a large number of men in the shops here. The Susquehanna division of our rail-road terminates here. The road was completed to this place in September, 1850. At this point the Hornellsville and Buffalo Rail-road commences, and will run in a direct course through the village of Attica to Buffalo. Its length is 90 miles. It is expected to be completed early in 1852. This will make a very direct route over our road from Buffalo to New York, between which points the distance will be 421½ miles. The population of Hornellsville is about 1000. What is called the "Western Division" of the road commences here. Leaving this station, following the course of the Caniacadea Creek, we soon commence the ascent to the summit between the waters of the Canisteo and Genesee Rivers, on a grade of 50 feet to the mile. Passing over a more expensive portion of the road than any we have seen for many miles, we enter a deep cut, and soon reach the station at

ALMOND (from New York 336½ miles, from Dunkirk 123½ miles). The village of Almond is prettily situated in the valley below, and contains about 1000 inhabitants. We here pass from Steuben into Allegany county. Just before reaching Almond the road turns suddenly from a westwardly course to one almost south, which it continues for about 15 miles.

BAKER'S BRIDGE (from New York 340½ miles, from Dunkirk 119½ miles) is a mere stopping-place, without depôt buildings, and only the shanties of the workmen around. About four miles from this station we reach Almond Summit, having attained an elevation of 1760 feet above tide-water, the highest point on the road.

ANDOVER (from New York 349 miles, from Dunkirk 111 miles) is a small village containing about 400 inhabitants, and is on one of the tributaries of the Genesee River. From this point the road resumes its westwardly course. The descent from the summit to this place is more moderate, being at the rate of 40 feet to the mile. This is a characteristic feature of the road, the grades opposed to the "direction of trade" being most moderate.

GENESEE (from New York 358 miles, from Dunkirk 102 miles). The village at this point is called Wellsville. It contains at present about 400 inhabitants; but its commanding position will insure it a large trade from the surrounding country. A plank road is about to be built to Cowdersport, the county town of Potter county, in Pennsylvania. Probably at no point on the road will so large a lumber trade be concentrated as here. At this point the road enters the Valley of the Genesee River, and follows the course of this beautiful stream, closely hugging its banks, for the next 10 miles. The course of the road is here again nearly north, along the valley of Dyke Creek, with easy grades to Genesee.

Scio (from New York 361½ miles, from Dunkirk 98½ miles) is a small village and station.

Phillipsburg (from New York 366 miles, from Dunkirk 94 miles) is the next station. The rail-road crosses the Genesee River here by a handsome bridge. The falls of the river afford very valuable water-power. Several saw-mills are in successful operation. An important lumber trade concentrates here. The village has the elements of a rapid and prosperous growth. Its population is about 600. It derives its name from the Hon. Philip Church, whose elegant residence, called Belvidere, stands on the east bank of the river. Mr. Church was originally the owner of a large territory in this neighborhood, much of which he still retains. The course of the road from Hornellsville to this point is very circuitous, to avoid which it was at one time proposed to construct a long tunnel, and thus save several miles in distance; but this was deemed inexpedient. The road has neither a tunnel, inclined plane, or draw-bridge, which, considering its great length, is rather remarkable.

Belvidere (from New York 369½ miles, from Dunkirk 90½ miles) is the next station we reach, and is pleasantly situated on the south side of the Genesee River, near the point where the road crosses that river, and follows up the course of one of its tributaries called Van Campen's Creek, so named after Major Moses Van Campen, who was a distinguished officer in the border war of the Revolution, and who died recently at Dansville, at the advanced age of 91 years. The village is well situated for trade with the adjoining towns of Angelica, Belfast, &c., and the northern part of Allegany county, and portions of Livingston and Wyoming, which will naturally strike the rail-road at this place. Here commences an ascent toward Cuba Summit of 30 feet to the mile. The pioneer settler of this region was Benjamin Chamberlain, who settled at Angelica. He was in the battles of Lexington and Bunker Hill, and was with Arnold at Quebec. He was a native of Massachusetts, and died at Angelica in 1847, aged 90 years.

FRIENDSHIP (from New York 374 miles, from Dunkirk 86 miles). This is the first station within the limits of the Holland Purchase, being in township No. 2, range No. 1. The village is healthy and pleasant, and is situated in the center of an excellent grazing country. Here is one of the most prosperous and well-conducted academies in the western part of the state. The population is about 500. About midway between this station and Cuba we reach what is called Cuba Summit, and commence the descent of 30 feet to the mile.

CUBA (from New York 383 miles, from Dunkirk 77 miles) is a lively business place, and has fair prospects of future growth. It is situated on Oil Creek, a tributary of the Alleghany. Here we first reach the waters that flow into the Mississippi. Oil Creek derives its name from a large spring situated five or six miles north of Cuba, from which large quantities of bituminous oil are obtained. A high value was set upon this oil by the Indians. Consequently, when by treaty they sold the western part of the state, they made a reservation around this spring of about one mile square, which is still owned by the Seneca nation, and is known on the maps as the Oil Spring Reservation. The population of Cuba is 800 or 900. Between this and the next station we pass into Cattaraugus county. Mr. Schoolcraft, in reference to the constant succession of hills and dales in this county, says they resemble a piece of rumpled calico. The village of Ellicottville, north of the road, occupies one of the deepest indentations or rumples. The name is derived from the Indian word Gar-ta-ra-ke-ras, signifying stinking shore or beach, originally applied to Lake Erie. This county is highly elevated, being from 500 to 1200 feet above Lake Erie. It was originally covered with a large amount of valuable timber and trees of lofty growth. Some of the trees have measured 230 feet in height, and five of them have been known to furnish a hundred "lumberman's" logs.

HINSDALE (from New York 388½ miles, from Dunkirk 71½ miles) is a small village, situated at the confluence of Oil and Ischua Creeks; and through the Valley of the Ischua, which extends north to the county of Erie, considerable business will probably come to this station. From this station to Olean the road runs near the Genesee Valley Canal, and crosses it near the latter place. The region is very pleasant, and the land fertile.

OLEAN (from New York 395 miles, from Dunkirk 65 miles). The station here is located about one mile northerly from the village of Olean, which is situated on the Alleghany River, and which we here see for the first time. At Olean were the earliest settlements made in this part of the country. Before the Holland Purchase Company had surveyed their lands and offered them for sale, Major Hoops, a Revolutionary officer, purchased a large tract of the proprietors at this place. Before the construction of the Erie Canal, Olean was the point through which the emigration for the South and West passed, and was for many years, for that reason, a place of much notoriety. The building of the canal and the establishment of steamboats on the lakes changed the order of things. The river at times remaining closed in the spring longer than was anticipated, the emigrants accumulated there in such numbers as to occasion a scarcity of food. Flour has sold on such occasions—say in 1818—as high as $25 per barrel, and pork as high as $50. Olean, in 1806, embraced the whole of Cattaraugus county; and James Green, who was the first supervisor, built a saw-mill in 1808, the first mill built for the lumber business on the Alleghany. Lumber was first taken down the river in 1808. In 1813 there was no white inhabitant on the Alleghany below Olean.

This station will receive the business of a large country

lying on the Upper Alleghany and its tributaries. The quantity of lumber in this neighborhood is very great, part of which will be sent east by rail-road, and part to the southwest by the Alleghany and Ohio, as formerly.

BURTON (from New York 399 miles, from Dunkirk 61 miles). This is the first station in the Valley of the Alleghany, and will receive the business of the valley of the Five-mile Run—a beautiful valley, as well as some part of the business of the Upper Alleghany. The road here follows closely the course of the Alleghany.

NINE-MILE CREEK (from New York 403 miles, from Dunkirk 57 miles) is at the eastern end of the Indian Reservation. The creek comes from a beautiful and fertile valley, which is rapidly increasing in population. The Alleghany Indian Reservation is about 30 miles long and one mile wide, extending both sides of the river. The hills inclosing the river are in some parts quite high, and the valley narrow. Occasionally the hills recede, and some excellent valley farms, occupied by the Indians, are to be seen, with good houses, barns, &c., and in a very creditable state of cultivation. The road passes through about 12 miles of the reservation.

GREAT VALLEY (from New York 411 miles, from Dunkirk 49 miles). This station is at the mouth of the creek of the same name, and is also on the Reservation, and commands the business of the valley, in which Ellicottville, the county seat, is situated. The Reservation belongs to the Seneca nation, who number about 700. The Alleghany, still in view, is the true Ohio, and is called Ohio by the Indians. The grade of the road here, and for several miles, is nearly level.

LITTLE VALLEY (from New York 422 miles, from Dunkirk 38 miles). At this place the business of Randolph, Jamestown, and other neighborhoods will concentrate. Here the road leaves the Alleghany River and the Indian Reservation, at the mouth of the Little Valley Creek, which stream it follows up some fifteen miles. The ascent from this point to the last summit before reaching Dunkirk, at Dayton, is easy.

ALBION (from New York 428½ miles, from Dunkirk 31½ miles) is a mere stopping-place.

DAYTON (from New York 437½ miles, from Dunkirk 22½ miles) is near the summit, between the waters flowing toward the Mississippi and Lake Erie. From this point to Dunkirk the descent is accomplished by various grades, the maximum being 40 feet per mile. The narrow glade between the dividing ridge and Lake Erie, from Cattaraugus Creek to the Pennsylvania line, gradually descends to the lake shore. The soil is gravelly, timbered with beach, sugar-maple, white-wood, hemlock, and pine, and yields abundant crops of grass, wheat, rye, corn, oats, barley, and esculent roots, and is well watered with numerous streams.

PERRYSBURG (from New York 440½ miles, from Dunkirk 19½ miles) is a small station.

SMITH'S MILLS (from New York 447½ miles, from Dunkirk 12½ miles). This is the last station in Cattaraugus county.

We enter Chautauque county—the last, not least, of the southern tier—at its eastern boundary, and pass through a highly-cultivated farming district, comprising the towns of Hanover, Sheridan, and Pomfret, to Lake Erie. The name of the county is a corruption of the Indian word Otsha-ta-ka, or, as others have it, Ja-da-queh, signifying *a land of mist*. The county was erected in 1808 by dividing Genesee. The commissioners, in locating the seat at Mayville, describe the place in general terms, and, as if to identify it by a permanent monument, add that they have planted in the center a large hemlock post. All the region between the Genesee River and the Pennsylvania line previous to 1800 was embraced in the town of Northampton, and the first tax-roll for that town bears date

H

October 6, 1800. The first white child born in Chautauque was John M'Henry, in 1802. He was drowned in Lake Erie while attempting to make a trip from the mouth of Chautauque Creek to Erie in a small boat after provisions. Chautauque Lake is a beautiful sheet of water, 20 miles long and from one to four wide. Its elevation is some 730 feet above Lake Erie, and 1300 feet above the level of the ocean, and it is said to be the highest navigable water on the continent. A steam-boat runs regularly upon it in summer, between Mayville and Jamestown.

Chautauque county, although in its infancy, has long since ceased to be a "secluded county." Bordering the lake, and with easy access to markets, its agricultural resources have been rapidly developing. Constant immigration from New England and the river country, and other portions of our state, have overspread it with a population of some 50,000, distinguished for their enterprise and intelligence. The table-lands bordering the lake produce all the grains, and the more hilly country back of them is mainly devoted to dairy purposes; and the butter and cheese produced in Chautauque are not far behind, in quality or quantity, any other county in the state. Dunkirk, Fredonia, Westfield, Mayville, Jamestown, Forestville, and Silver Creek are the principal villages. The first station on the road in the county, as we approach the lake, is

HANOVER (from New York $451\frac{1}{2}$ miles, from Dunkirk $8\frac{1}{2}$ miles), near the beautiful village of Forestville. Hanover station will accommodate the local business of several towns, and soon grow into a flourishing village. Just after leaving the station we cross Walnut Creek, deriving its name from a black walnut tree, a giant of the forest, that grew on its banks near the village of Silver Creek, so immense in its proportions as to attract the attention of travelers. In about 1825 it fell to the ground. Off from the hollow butt was cut some 18 feet in length, which was neatly roofed over, and arranged for a saloon, so as to accommodate some ten or twelve at a time; and this curious structure was brought East, and exhibited in the Atlantic cities, and afterward transported to Europe, and there displayed in London, Paris, and elsewhere abroad; and, by way of take-off upon the extravagances of European tourists in this country, it was represented to be a fair specimen of the forest trees in America. The eye of the traveler soon looks out upon the broad blue waters of Lake Erie, and a pleasant run from Hanover, through fertile fields dotted over with comfortable dwellings, soon brings him to the termination of this "more than Appian Way," at Dunkirk, where ample arrangements are in progress to send the traveler on his way. Lines of first-class steam-boats will receive, in summer time, such as are weary of rail-road travel, and speed them westward, while the more impetuous and impatient of delay, or those who shrink from the dangers and perils of the sea, will take the Lake-shore Rail-road, now rapidly progressing to completion.

There are numerous inflammable gas springs in this county, some of which have been applied to practical and beneficial purposes, the stores, hotels, and public buildings in Fredonia (a pleasant and thriving village three miles south of Dunkirk) being lighted by the supply derived from one which issues from the bed of the Canadaway Creek, and the light-house at Barcelona (16 miles from Dunkirk) being also lighted from a supply obtained in its vicinity. It is quite probable that, ere long, "natural gas," as it is commonly called, will be brought into more general use.

There are likewise numerous mineral springs in this county, some of which, and particularly those in Dunkirk and its vicinity, are held in very high repute, an analysis having shown them to possess superior medicinal properties.

DUNKIRK (from New York 460 miles). This terminus of the road upon the lake is destined to a rapid growth into one of the flourishing cities of the Lakes. It is not without some share of early renown. In 1815 or thereabouts, a military road, to be constructed by the state through the southern tier of counties, was projected by De Witt Clinton and others, and, after a personal examination of the lake-shore between Buffalo and Erie, the Harbor of Dunkirk, then called Chadwick's Bay, was selected as the contemplated termination of the great public high-way. Subsequently, impressed with the idea of its value as a harbor, De Witt Clinton, Colonel Elisha Jenkins, Messrs. I. and J. Townsend, and others, of Albany, bought land for the site of a town, and laid out a village, and called it Dunkirk, after some town in France Colonel Jenkins had seen in his travels, as he thought, resembling it. The county was at that time a wilderness; the waves of Erie washed a solitary shore; all improvement was conjectural; and the future, so full of wonders, was veiled form their view; and it is no slight compliment to the sagacity and forecast of these early pioneers of Dunkirk, that all subsequent examinations and experience have vindicated their wisdom, and established the correctness of their conjectures respecting it.

Government erected a light-house on the western point, which affords the western protection of the bay, in 1824; and subsequently a beacon-light at the main channel, and a breakwater across the bay, having expended some $80,000, which, for want of further expenditure, has gone greatly to decay. All careful and minute examination and surveys by the engineer corps of the government and of the rail-road company, so much interested in forming the best possible lake connection, have established the fact that the harbor is capacious, accessible, secure, and capable of improvement to one of the best, if not the very best, upon the Lakes.

The village now contains about 1500 inhabitants. The rail-road company are making ample preparations for a large freight and passenger business at this point. Individual enterprise is also concerned and active to develop the advantages of that lake connection; improvements are rapidly progressing to meet the requirements of business, and it needs no sagacity to foresee that Dunkirk will shoot up as if by magic into a commercial town of vast importance.

The site is a beautiful one. The ground gradually rises as it recedes from the lake, so that at one mile from the shore it is about 100 feet above the level of the water. There are no local diseases, but the climate is delightful. In summer time the cool breeze from the lake is constantly playing; the sunsets are as glowing and beautiful as those of Italy; the mornings are bright and lovely. There can be no more agreeable place for residence; and the business advantages of the town will necessarily mainly attract there enterprising men from all quarters; and a populous town will soon take the place of the present somewhat obscure village of Dunkirk, and ranges of lofty blocks, and cupolas, and spires, and masts of tall ships, will ere long be reflected in the glassy surface of her great bay.

A rail-road from Buffalo to Dunkirk is in progress, and another from Dunkirk to Erie, Pennsylvania, 50 miles distant. Many months will not elapse before there will be a continuous rail-road from New York to Cincinnati and to Chicago; and within two years a journey may be made from New York to the Mississippi in less time than was occupied 25 years ago in traveling from Boston to New York.

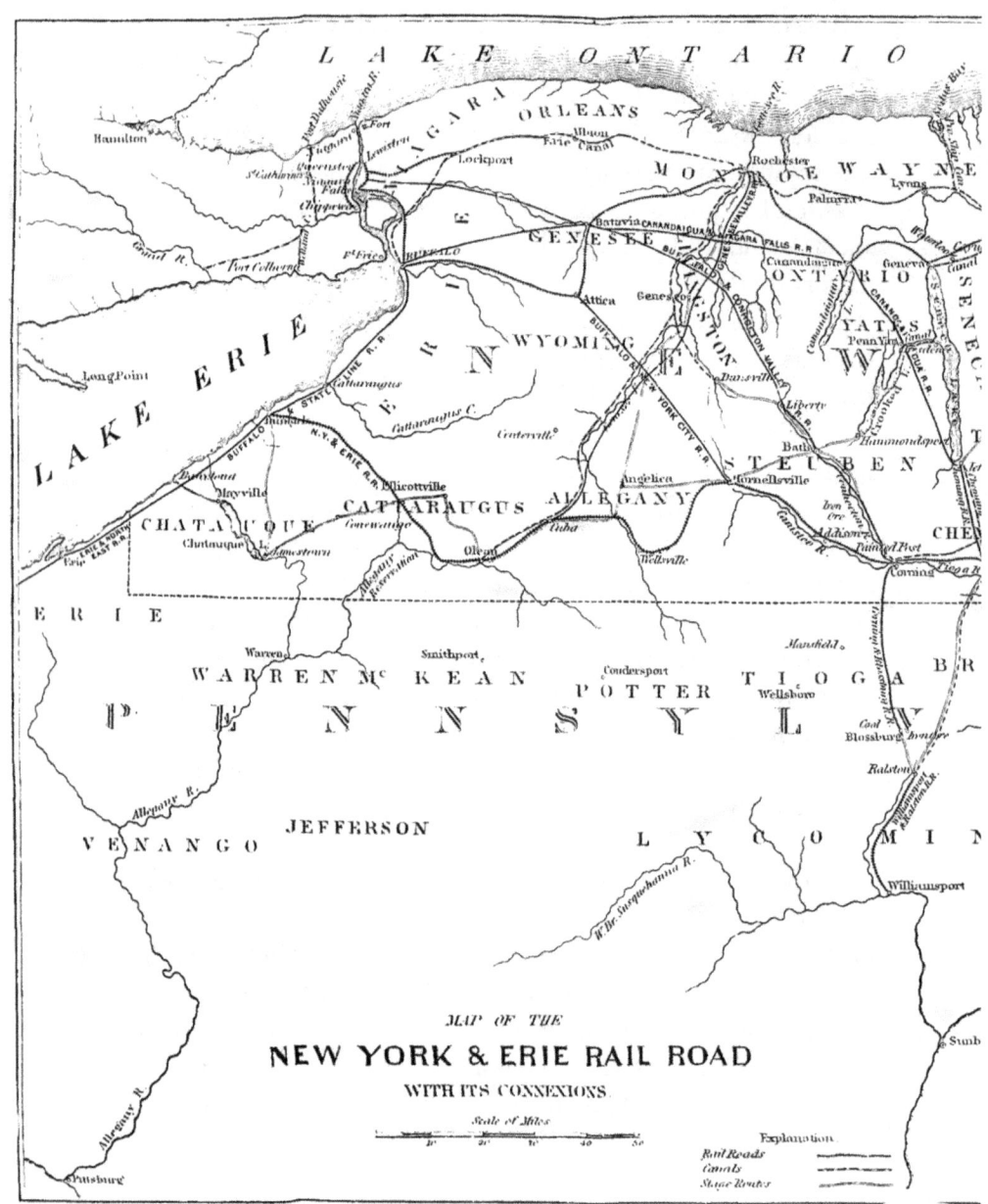

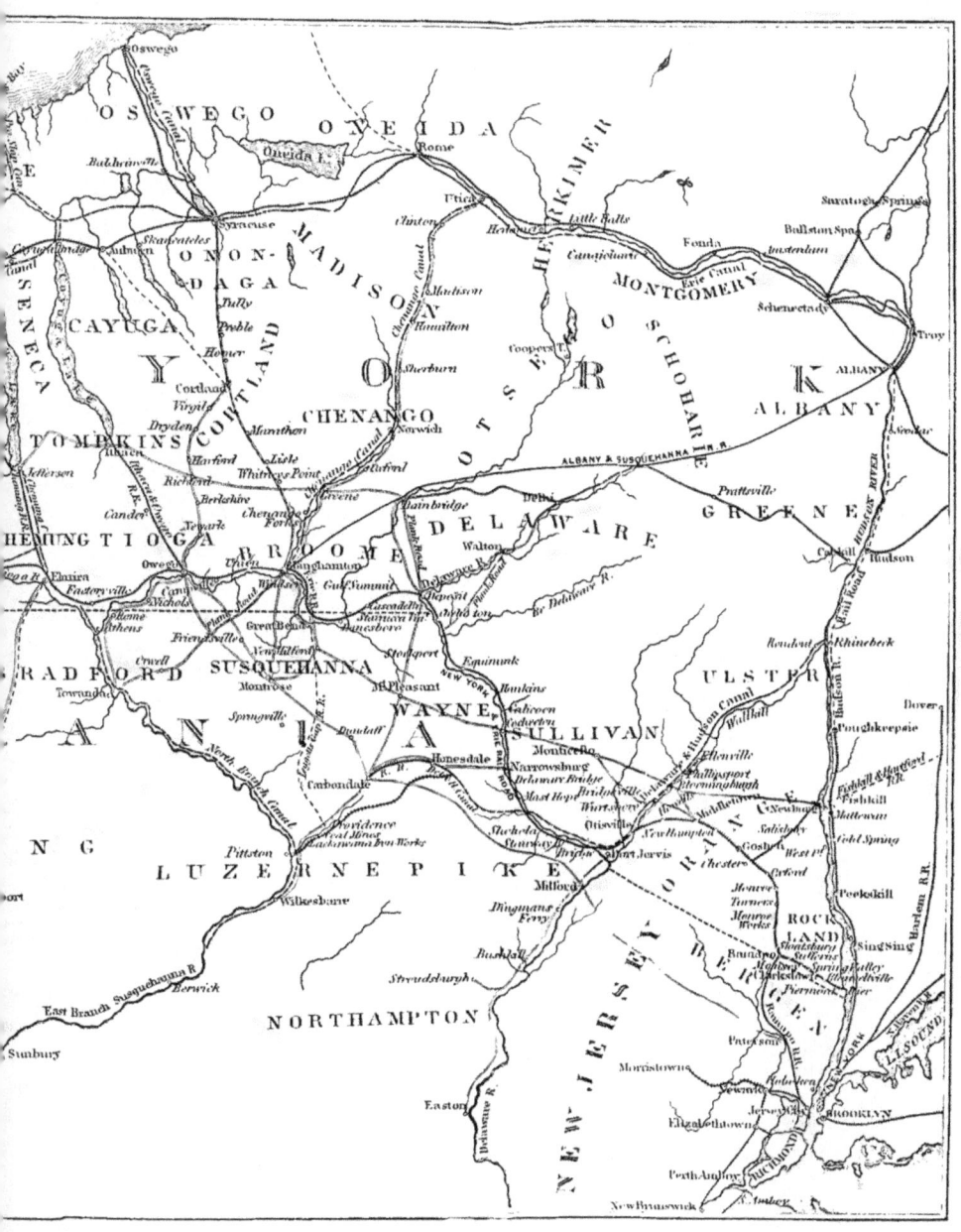

# TABLE OF DISTANCES.

| | Dist. from New York | Dist. from Dunkirk | | Dist. from New York | Dist. from Dunkirk |
|---|---|---|---|---|---|
| New York | | 460 m. | Campville | 230 m. | 230 m. |
| Aquackanonck | 12 m. | 448 " | Owego | 236½ " | 223½ " |
| Paterson | 16 " | 444 " | Tioga Center | 242 " | 218 " |
| Suffern's | 32 " | 428 " | Smithborough | 246 " | 214 " |
| Ramapo Works | 34 " | 426 " | Barton | 249 " | 211 " |
| Sloatsburg | 35½ " | 424½ " | Waverley | 255½ " | 204½ " |
| Monroe Works | 42 " | 418 " | Chemung | 260½ " | 199½ " |
| Wilkes's | 44 " | 416 " | Wellsburg | 266 " | 194 " |
| Turner's | 47 " | 413 " | Elmira | 273 " | 187 " |
| Monroe | 49½ " | 410½ " | Junction | 277 " | 183 " |
| Oxford | 52 " | 408 " | Big Flat | 283 " | 177 " |
| Chester | 55 " | 405 " | Corning | 291 " | 169 " |
| Goshen | 59½ " | 400½ " | Painted Post | 292 " | 168 " |
| New Hampton | 63½ " | 396½ " | Addison | 301½ " | 158½ " |
| Middletown | 67 " | 393 " | Rathboneville | 306½ " | 153½ " |
| Howell's | 71 " | 389 " | Cameron | 314 " | 146 " |
| Otisville | 75½ " | 385½ " | Canisteo | 326 " | 134 " |
| Shin Hollow | 82 " | 378 " | Hornellsville | 331½ " | 128½ " |
| Delaware | 88 " | 372 " | Almond | 336½ " | 123½ " |
| Rosa Switch | 98 " | 362 " | Baker's Bridge | 340½ " | 119½ " |
| Barryville | 107 " | 353 " | Andover | 349 " | 111 " |
| Lackawaxen | 111 " | 349 " | Genesee | 358 " | 102 " |
| Mast Hope | 116 " | 344 " | Scio | 361½ " | 98½ " |
| Narrowsburgh | 122 " | 338 " | Phillipsburg | 365½ " | 94½ " |
| Cochecton | 130½ " | 329½ " | Belvidere | 369 " | 91 " |
| Callicoon | 136 " | 324 " | Friendship | 373½ " | 86½ " |
| Hankin's | 143 " | 317 " | Cuba | 382½ " | 77½ " |
| Equinunk | 153 " | 307 " | Hinsdale | 388 " | 72 " |
| Stockport | 159 " | 301 " | Olean | 395 " | 65 " |
| Hancock | 163½ " | 296½ " | Burton | 399 " | 61 " |
| Hale's Eddy | 171½ " | 288½ " | Nine-mile Creek | 403 " | 57 " |
| Deposit | 176½ " | 283½ " | Great Valley | 411 " | 49 " |
| Summit | 184 " | 276 " | Little Valley | 421½ " | 38½ " |
| Susquehanna | 192 " | 268 " | Albion | 428½ " | 31½ " |
| Great Bend | 200½ " | 259½ " | Dayton | 437½ " | 22½ " |
| Kirkwood | 206 " | 254 " | Perrysburg | 440½ " | 19½ " |
| Windsor Road | 210 " | 250 " | Smith's Mills | 447½ " | 12½ " |
| Binghamton | 215 " | 245 " | Hanover | 451½ " | 8½ " |
| Union | 223 " | 237 " | Dunkirk | 460 " | 0 |

THE END.

## Reprinted by
## New York History Review Press

Why do we digitally restore and reprint vintage books?

***Plain and simple - if we don't, who will?*** We believe a digitally restored book should have the appearance that it would have had if it never needed mending. It should have as much of the original material as is possible to use and still maintain the usability of the book. All new work should be in keeping with the style and the time in which the book was produced.

Our conservators maintain the integrity of the book while making it usable in the present, and preserving the content for posterity. Digital methods have made the art of book restoration a much simpler task, allowing restoration artists to work on a digital image instead of the original photograph, slide or negative. Our books have been restored to an excellent state without altering the original concept. Old books can be revived by "cleaning up" mildew, water stains, spots, and tears.

Our printing method uses state of the art technology and the Internet provides 24/7 worldwide access to find these fine old books.

Thank you for your interest!

NewYorkHistoryReview.com

www.ingramcontent.com/pod-product-compliance
Lightning Source LLC
Chambersburg PA
CBHW032257150426
43195CB00008BA/489